The Language of Interpretation

NCTE Research Report No. 27

The Language
of Interpretation

Patterns of Discourse
in Discussions of Literature

James D. Marshall
University of Iowa

Peter Smagorinsky
University of Oklahoma

Michael W. Smith
Rutgers University

In collaboration with

Helen Dale, Richard H. Fehlman, Pamela K. Fly, Ruth A. Frawley, Suzanne E. Gitomer, Mary Beth Hines, David E. Wilson

National Council of Teachers of English
1111 W. Kenyon Road, Urbana, Illinois 61801-1096

Staff Editors: Sheila A. Ryan and David Hamburg

Interior Book Design: Tom Kovacs for TGK Design

NCTE Stock Number: 27096-3050

Library of Congress Cataloging-in-Publication Data

Marshall, James D., 1950–
    The language of interpretation : patterns of discourse in
  discussions of literature / James D. Marshall, Peter Smagorinsky,
  Michael W. Smith, in collaboration with Helen Dale . . . [et al.].
     p. cm.
  Includes bibliographical references and index.
  ISBN 0-8141-2709-6
  1. Discourse analysis. 2. Literature—Study and teaching.
I. Smagorinsky, Peter. II. Smith, Michael W. (Michael William),
1954–   . III. Title.
P302.M377 1995
809'.0071—dc20   94-26194
                                        CIP

Contents

Acknowledgments

We would like to thank a number of people who have been instrumental in the development of this project. First of all, we would like to thank the many teachers, students, and adult readers who so generously allowed us into their classrooms and homes to collect the data analyzed in these studies. Their cooperation and the risks they took in allowing their discussions to be analyzed so critically have earned from us our greatest respect, admiration, and appreciation.

We would especially like to thank the teacher-researchers who interviewed their colleagues, transcribed many of our videotaped large-group discussions, and helped us think through the issues we were exploring. These included Susan Burke, Ann Connolly, John Danaher, Roseanne DeFabio, Carol Forman-Pemberton, Tricia Hansbury, David Marhafer, and Doris Quick.

We would also like to acknowledge several funding sources for supporting this work. The research reported in Chapter 3 was supported by grants from the Research Foundation of the National Council of Teachers of English, from the U.S. Department of Education, Office of Educational Research and Improvement, and from the National Endowment for the Arts and was conducted in conjunction with the Center for the Learning and Teaching of Literature. The research reported in Chapter 4 was supported with resources provided by the Department of Instructional Leadership and Academic Curriculum and the Information Processing Service at the University of Oklahoma. The research reported in Chapters 5 and 6 was supported with a Graduate School Summer Grant from the University of Wisconsin–Madison.

We would like to thank our former and present graduate students who assisted with the data collection and analysis: Richard Fehlman, Mary Beth Hines, and David Wilson for Chapter 3; Pam Fly for Chapter 4; Helen Dale for Chapters 5 and 6; and Ruth Frawley and Suzanne Gitomer for Chapter 6. We would also like to thank the colleagues who gave us valuable feedback on the manuscript: Helen Dale, Anne DiPardo, Pam Fly, Steve Gevinson, Mary Beth Hines, and Brian White. Thanks go as well to the outside reviewers and Editorial Board of NCTE for their careful reading of the text and to Michael Spooner for his sterling work in coordinating the whole effort. We greatly appreciate their contributions to the final shape of this monograph.

Finally, we would like to thank our families for their support during the development of this project. We dedicate this book to them with great love and appreciation for their contributions to our work and with our most sincere thanks for their tolerance of our working.

1 Introduction

A teacher and her ninth-grade students have for several days been discussing Dickens's *Great Expectations*. The discussion has been slow and sometimes tedious; the students are quite clearly bored. Hoping to find a new way to approach the discussion, the teacher takes a moment to ask her students how they feel about the way things have been going:

> *Teacher:* . . . So let's take a moment to talk about how our discussions have been working lately.
>
> *Terry:* I don't know how anybody else feels, but I do not like picking apart a book. We could spend an entire period on just one page. It just makes the book a lot less enjoyable.
>
> *Jenny:* Yeah, this isn't a lab or something.
>
> *Teacher:* Putting it under the microscope.
>
> *Brian:* Yeah, that's true, because it gets sort of boring after a while. I read it and I understand it and then, but why do we have to go over it?
>
> *Teacher:* All right, some of you understand and want to get on with it and others find the discussion helps in understanding. Tony, something you want to add?
>
> *Tony:* I just don't care for the book. I think it's boring.
>
> *Teacher:* You're not pleased with the book.
>
> *Tony:* And doing it over and over and over again doesn't help.
>
> *Teacher:* That's enough. All right. I hear you, and we'll see what we can do about it. But for today, let's go on precisely the way we were. . . .

In many ways the studies we report in this book are an attempt to understand what has happened in this brief classroom episode. Why have the discussions so far taken the particular shape they have? Why do the students find them boring? Why, in spite of everyone's frustration, does the teacher decide to go on "precisely the way we were"? What other ways of proceeding might be available to her?

To explore these questions, we undertook a series of studies examining the ways in which people talk about literature in a variety of contexts. Our purpose in this book is to describe as fully as we can how discussions of literature proceed, to explore the intentions and expectations of those who participate in such discussions, and to use our analyses as the basis of a consideration of what constitutes effective instruction. We hope that our efforts will provoke conversations among teachers as they reflect upon their practice and that they will provide one point of departure for future study of the teaching and learning of literature. Although we focus primarily on the kinds of discussions that take place in school, we are interested as well in talk about literature that takes place outside the classroom and, more generally, in how talk about literature helps shape participants' response to the texts that they read.

A full-scale study of the language that readers use to discuss literature seems especially relevant now as work in both reading and literary theory has converged on the concept of "constructive processes" in describing the act of reading. Though drawing from a variety of theoretical perspectives, this research has explained the process of reading as a transaction between the language on the page and the purposes, expectations, and prior knowledge of the reader. Given this model, it seems important to ask if and how *discussions* of literature help shape reader-text transactions by fostering specific ways of talking and thinking about texts. As Bruner and Olson (1980) have argued, knowledge is acquired through activity; in their aphorism, by sitting on chairs, we learn both about "chairs" and about "sitting." By the same token, talking about literature may provide readers with knowledge about literature. But it will also provide knowledge about the conventional ways of talking about literature: the language, questions, and responses that are thought to be appropriate in given contexts and those that are thought to be less so. Discussions of literature, in other words, may constitute a kind of tacit curriculum in conventional modes of literary knowledge—a curriculum about which we know very little.

Literature and Schooling

The study of literature in school has from the start been marked by tensions concerning the kinds of conventions that ought to prevail and about the kinds of literary knowledge teachers ought to foster. As early as 1892, Professor Francis March, in an address to the Modern Language Association, noted that the young profession was

> having an outcry . . . against stopping to study particular passages in literature, urging rapid emotional reading, the seeking to produce love of reading rather than knowledge of books—love of reading all the new magazines, I suppose, and newspapers, and novels . . . instead of spending days and nights with the great authors. . . . Professors who aim at the highest usefulness and the most honored position must labor to give profound knowledge and excite lasting love of great books and devotion to great thoughts. . . . Their literary studies must be mainly upon great authors. (1893, p. 27)

March's representation of professional divisions in the teaching of literature seems remarkably clear. On the one hand are the close reading of particular passages, "profound knowledge," "lasting love," and "great books." On the other hand are "rapid emotional reading," "love of reading," and "new magazines . . . newspapers, and novels." The representation places a knowledge of books in conflict with a love of books, careful reading in conflict with emotional reading, literature that has lasted in conflict with literature that is new. March left little doubt as to where his own loyalties lay, but his description of tensions already present in the teaching of literature one hundred years ago foreshadowed the kinds of debates that have continued ever since.

The year 1938 marked a turning point in those debates, for in that year two books that were to have an enormous impact on the teaching of literature were published. The first of these was *Understanding Poetry,* Cleanth Brooks and Robert Penn Warren's seminal collection of poetry and critical commentary that is usually cited as one of the anchoring documents of the New Criticism. In *Understanding Poetry,* Brooks and Warren laid out a set of principles that, in their view, should guide the reading and analysis of literature. In the book's opening statement—a statement they frame as a "Letter to the Teacher"— Brooks and Warren forwarded an approach that helped to shape the teaching of literature for decades to follow:

> This book has been conceived on the assumption that if poetry is worth teaching at all, it is worth teaching as poetry. The poem in itself . . . remains finally the object for study. One must grasp the poem as a literary construct before it can offer any real illumination as a document. [In the teaching of literature] the treatment should be concrete and inductive, [and] the poem should be treated as an organic system of relationships. (pp. iv–xv)

With words such as "organic," "concrete," "construct," and "object," Brooks and Warren provided a vocabulary for discussing literature and the teaching of literature that emphasized literature's formal, objective characteristics and that deemphasized the importance of both the author and the reader. They were attempting, in other words, to construct an intellectually coherent and systematically objective method for reading and teaching texts—a method that would produce accurate, sound, defensible interpretations. Drawing heavily from the positivistic assumptions of the natural sciences, Brooks and Warren were trying to make the study of texts similar to the study of other phenomena. If texts are defined as objective, organic constructs, then close reading can be defined as the detached, objective analysis of those constructs. Studying literature, in this view, can be understood as comparable to studying biology or physics. The object of study is different, of course, but the method—the close, inductive investigation of parts and wholes—is similar. Poetry, Brooks and Warren argued, is not at all like scientific writing; but criticism of poetry should probably aim for the same kind of clear-headed, objective analysis that we find in the best scientific inquiry.

It was, and it remains, a powerful argument. But it was only the first of two important statements about the teaching of literature that were to appear in 1938. The second was Louise Rosenblatt's *Literature as Exploration*. A disciple of John Dewey, Rosenblatt was writing at a time when progressive thought about education was rich and lively, and she opened her book with a very different agenda from that of Brooks and Warren. "In a turbulent age," she wrote,

> our schools and colleges must prepare the student to meet unprecedented and unpredictable problems. He needs to understand himself; he needs to work out harmonious relationships with other people. He must achieve a philosophy, an inner center from which to view in perspective the shifting society about him; he will influence for good or ill its future development. Any knowledge about man and society that schools can give him should be assimilated into the stream of his actual life. (p. 3)

Whereas Brooks and Warren open their volume with a discussion of what poetry is, Rosenblatt begins hers with a discussion of what students need. Whereas Brooks and Warren are at pains to say what a text is so that we might bring ourselves into a proper relationship with it, Rosenblatt is at pains to say who students are so that texts may be brought into proper relationship with them. For Rosenblatt, reading literature is not objective analysis, but an exploration, a process, an experience in which readers draw upon their own histories, their own emotions, in order to, quite literally, make sense of the text. Meaning for Rosenblatt is not found in the text; it is made by the reader in transaction with the text.

These transactions, these efforts to make sense of texts, will result in different readings from different readers, making arguments about the objective meaning of a text problematic, and making certainty about those meanings virtually impossible. A classroom emphasizing such transactions would be one in which readings are shared and explored and where students and teachers develop their associations with each other as well as with the texts under study. It would be a classroom, in other words, that would model the kind of democratic community that Dewey hoped to foster. Rosenblatt's perspective is clearly very different from that offered by Brooks and Warren—so different, in fact, that we may be surprised that the two perspectives were articulated in the very same year. That they were suggests that the professional tensions described by Francis March in his 1892 MLA address had not been resolved even fifty years after the event.

Those tensions remained, of course, but after 1938 and most especially after 1945, when the universities were flooded with returning soldiers, the assumptions and critical procedures proposed by Brooks and Warren under the rubric of the New Criticism gained a nearly universal ascendancy in schools. Those assumptions and procedures were supported in part by the enormous prestige enjoyed by the natural sciences in mid-century and by the influence of the scientific method on almost every discipline. But what made the New Criticism so successful was not simply its implicit identification with scientific objectivity. Its case was helped enormously by the fact that it worked in classrooms (Ohmann, 1976; Eagleton, 1983; Graff, 1990). Students could be trained to do close readings, and they did not have to spend years examining the life of the author or the historical period of the text to do so. What was important about literature, the New Critics argued, was in the text. It was there for anyone to read, and almost anyone could be taught to do so.

The New Criticism, then, was not just scientific, it was, in its own way, democratic: almost anyone could be taught to do a close reading. Perhaps just as important for its popularity in schools, close reading in the New Critical tradition was a skill that could be evaluated. Readings could be judged as good, bad, or indifferent by a clear criterion of accuracy—by how adequately those readings accounted for the objective reality of the text itself. In a sense, then, the New Criticism mapped so neatly onto some of the conventions of schooling that it almost seemed as if the two had been made for each other. The New Criticism was not just a way of reading literature, it was a way of teaching literature, and, at least through the 1960s, the kinds of critical procedures proposed by literary scholars and the kinds of instructional proce-dures practiced by literature teachers shared a set of assumptions that effec-tively governed the production and consumption of knowledge in literary studies.

That set of shared assumptions among scholars and teachers has begun to unravel in the last two decades as reader-oriented developments in literary theory have brought into question many of the premises of the New Criticism. As Mailloux (1982) has argued, such reader-oriented critics

> focus on readers in the act of reading. Some examine individual readers through psychological observations and participation; others discuss reading communities through philosophical speculation and literary in-tuition. . . . All share the . . . assumption that it is impossible to separate perceiver from perceived, subject from object. Thus they reject the text's autonomy, its absolute separateness, in favor of its dependence on the reader's creation or participation. Perception is viewed as interpretive; reading is not the discovery of meaning but the creation of it. Reader-response criticism replaces examinations of a text in-and-of-itself with discussions of the reading process, the "interaction" of reader and text. (p. 20)

By focusing on the reader and the text in transaction, rather than on the "text-in-and-of itself," reader-response theorists have raised a range of new questions about how literary texts can be known. The questions address, among others, issues of gender (Fetterley, 1978; Tompkins, 1985), ethnicity (Gates, 1988; Lee, 1993), psychology (Bleich, 1975; Holland, 1975), and culture (Fish, 1980; Scholes, 1985). If readers are actively involved in the construction of literary meaning, then readers and the contexts surrounding readers are as important to the literary transaction as the texts to which the readers are responding. The most basic critical question in this view is not "What does this text mean?" but "How can this text be read?" and the answer to that question will depend ultimately on who is doing the reading and on what makes up the context of reading.

Language in the Classroom

One of the most important contexts in which students learn how to read texts, of course, is the classroom. And in the classroom, readings are shaped primarily through discussion. If we are to understand what students are learning about literature, then, we must understand the nature of classroom discussion.

At least two traditions of scholarship have examined classroom talk. The first has provided detailed and consistent descriptions of how classroom talk proceeds. Beginning with Flanders's (Amidon & Flanders, 1963) use of "interaction analysis" in the early 1960s and extending through a range of studies in a variety of instructional settings (Barnes, 1969; Bellack, Kleibard, Hyman, & Smith, 1966; Cazden, 1988; Mehan, 1979; Sinclair & Coulthard, 1975), this tradition has characterized classroom talk as a linguistic register with very specific conventions. In brief, discourse in classrooms seems to move fairly consistently in a three-turn pattern of teacher question–student response– teacher evaluation, a pattern Mehan (1979) described as initiation, response, evaluation (I/R/E). The questions tend to be closed rather than open, inviting factual or literal answers rather than answers requiring extensive reasoning or evaluation. Teachers provide the structure for discussions, orchestrating beginnings, conclusions, and topic shifts. In general, as Barnes (1969) has argued, such patterns suggest strongly that a "transmission model" of teaching and learning prevails in schools, with teachers providing the information that students are to absorb, and with students allowed little room to bring their own knowledge or language to bear on that information.

The transmission model of communication, with its assumption that a message can move intact from a sender to a passive receiver, is problematic if not naíve. In focusing on the message and the sender, it ignores the constructive way in which people interpret messages. If Rosenblatt is right in arguing that the reader's or receiver's characteristics affect the way in which meaning is constructed from texts and messages, then the transmission model badly underestimates the activity of the receiver in making sense of a message.

Nonetheless, as countless observers of classrooms have noted (e.g., Dillon & Searle, 1981; Goodlad, 1984; Nystrand & Gamoran, 1991a), the transmission model prevails in American schools. A different perspective, however, has offered a powerful framework for understanding how talk may come to shape students' knowledge of the subjects they study in school, including literature. The work of Bakhtin (1981, 1984, 1986), Berger and Luckmann (1966), Vygotsky (1978, 1986), Wertsch (1985, 1991), and others has forwarded a view of learning that stresses the social influences on the ways in which people think. This view sees thinking as being shaped by the environment in which an individual develops, with language being among the primary mediators of learning in the environment. In most societies, language plays a crucial mediating role in the ways people internalize the norms, categories, patterns of thought, and values of a culture. Stated simply, in most cultures people learn how to think by listening to—and participating in—the ways in which the people around them talk.

In school, people talk in very particular ways. Schools are among the settings "where certain patterns of speaking and thinking are easier, or come to be viewed as more appropriate . . . than others" (Wertsch, 1991, p. 38). Bakhtin (1986) refers to these more appropriate patterns of speaking and thinking as "speech genres" and says that they become "privileged," or widely and perhaps dogmatically accepted as the "right" way of communicating in particular settings.

What these language theorists have made clear is the stakes of the game. In studying classroom discourse, we are studying more than just recitation patterns; we are studying the processes through which the participants learn and perpetuate appropriate ways of knowing in classrooms. And what happens in classrooms affects for many students their sense of self-worth, their prospects for future success in school and career, and their belief in the value of formal learning.

The Project

Our studies of discussions of literature, then, proceed from the instructional challenges presented by new, reader-oriented developments in literary theory and from powerful models of learning that may enable us to develop richer and more deeply reasoned portraits of the complex relationships between thinking and speaking. We believe strongly that the models of teaching literature that have prevailed in schools for almost half a century must be reimagined in light of new theory and new scholarship and that a clear view of current practice may be a helpful place to begin that larger project. As we explain in the next chapter, we have brought together our research in three complementary areas in order to help begin that portrait.

2 A Description of the Project

Our studies examine the nature of talk about literature in three contexts: (1) teacher-led large groups, (2) teacher-orchestrated small groups, and (3) adults and adolescents talking about literature outside classrooms. We have chosen to study talk about literature in these settings because they represent, we think, the most likely contexts in which discussions of literature will take place.

Three central questions guided our research:

1. What are the basic patterns of talk about literature in these three contexts?

2. What assumptions about teaching, learning, language, and literature inform that talk?

3. What are the important similarities and differences in the patterns of talk and in the purposes for talk in these three contexts?

Though each of our studies addresses these questions, our monograph differs from most in NCTE's Research Report series in that our studies were not conceived together as related elements of a unified project. Rather, as our understanding of discourse evolved, we began to recognize the connections among our research interests. Before we detail the studies we will be presenting, therefore, it seems to us worthwhile to take a short detour to explain how we brought our work together.

Beginnings

Jim Marshall's studies of large-group discussions of literature are an outgrowth of interests he developed while doing his dissertation and provided in many ways the impetus for the other studies we report. Jim's dissertation (Marshall, 1987) details how the language of the classroom affects the nature of students' written and oral responses. Jim undertook the studies we report in Chapter 3 to take a more comprehensive look at the language of literary interpretation as practiced in schools and what the effects of that language might be. With a grant from the Center for the Learning and Teaching of Literature at SUNY–Albany, he spent a summer with six teacher-researchers,

who were themselves studying classroom discussions. Working from interviews with teachers and students and from transcripts of classroom discussions, Jim developed the coding system that we have adopted here. His
experiences revealed to him a number of tensions that seem to inform classroom discussions and the teaching of literature more generally, tensions that
led him to pursue his research on literary discourse in further studies.

Michael Smith first heard Jim present his work at the Midwinter Conference of the Assembly for Research. This conference is different from most in
its small size (usually fewer than one hundred people attend) and in its
emphasis on conversation (at several times during the conference the speakers
and audience break out into discussion groups to talk about the papers the
speakers have presented). Often conversations begun in these groups spill
over into other venues as conference participants share meals or drinks. After
hearing Jim's presentation, Michael was struck by how the intellectual engagement and enjoyment that characterized the talk among adults at the
conference was so often absent in the discussions Jim had studied. Although
classrooms and conferences are decidedly different contexts, noting that contrast inspired Michael to look outside classrooms for settings that might
provide teachers an alternative model for talk about texts. And because he
wanted to be able to compare those discussions to the ones Jim studied, it
made sense for him to use the same method of analysis.

Jim became aware of Peter Smagorinsky's research on the relationship
between teacher-led and small-group discussions of literature when he re-
viewed a grant proposal that Peter had written. Peter's research built on Jim's
work by looking at one alternative to teacher-led discussions that Jim had
recommended—small-group discussions—to investigate the extent to which
they foster different types of discourse than characteristically occur in teacher-
led discussions. Peter chose to adopt Jim's method of data analysis to enable
him to situate his findings in a larger context. Because the value of small
groups was a point of discussion in the high school where Peter was teaching,
he enlisted several of his colleagues to join him in a teacher-research project
that examined how students talked in large- and small-group settings, with
particular attention to the relationships among the patterns of discourse between the two settings.

So although our studies were originally developed to be reported separately, they are all informed by the beliefs we articulate in Chapter 1 and use
the same method of analysis. In that the three of us were friends to begin with
and looked forward to the opportunity to learn more about our work by
bringing it together, we decided to write this book. The studies are not,
however, cut from exactly the same cloth. Jim's study is a comprehensive
analysis of large-group discussions, while Peter's and Michael's studies are
exploratory and consequently smaller in scope. Jim's and Michael's studies

include interview data and Peter's does not, in part because Peter would need to have interviewed himself in order to include such a component in his study; and though he is often accused of talking to himself, he thought it wise not to make such conversations public. Consequently, there will be some differences in the ways the studies are reported. As we have said, however, we believe the relationships among the studies diminish the problems caused by these methodological differences. Our efforts to identify those relationships were greatly aided by our using the same coding system in each of our studies. We next explain the features of that coding system, a system we use to analyze the transcripts of literary discussions reported in Chapters 3, 4, 5, and 6.

Method of Analysis

To examine the basic features of the discussions we studied, we used the coding system Jim had developed for his studies (Marshall, 1989). It distinguishes two levels of organization: speaker turns, which included everything a speaker said before yielding the floor; and communication units, which were statements within speaker turns that were coded for analysis. We analyzed each communication unit for linguistic function, for knowledge base, and for kind of reasoning. In the following section we provide an overview of the system for coding the communication units in the transcripts. Because the meaning of individual statements is clear only in the context of the discussions in which they are made, we illustrate the coding system with extended transcripts in the appendix, rather than with isolated statements in the sections that follow.

Organization of Discussions

In order to mark the boundaries that shape classroom discussions, each transcribed discussion was first segmented at two levels: communication unit and turn.

> **Communication Unit:** The basic unit of analysis, communication units have the force of a sentence, though may be as short as one word (for example, "yes" or "okay"). They represent an identifiable remark or utterance on a single subject.
>
> **Turn:** The most obvious boundary in most oral discourse, a turn consists of one or more communication units spoken by a single participant who holds the floor.

Transcripts were further divided into *episodes,* the largest segments of discourse analyzed. Episodes represent a sequence of speaker turns on a single, identifiable topic. To avoid confusion about the duration of episodes, episode boundaries were marked only when one of the participants made an explicit move to do so, such as when a teacher told students to move on to a new point.

The Language of Discussions

In order to examine the linguistic patterns and intellectual content of class-room discussions, each communication unit was coded within one of five basic categories and within one of several subcategories that allowed a closer analysis of its features. The major categories and their respective subcategories are explained below.

  I. *Direct:* any remark (even when it is represented as a question) that intends to move others (usually students) toward an action or to shift their attention or the focus on the discussion
 II. *Inform:* any statement of fact or opinion whose purpose is to represent what the speaker knows, believes, or thinks about a topic. Reading and quoting from texts are included here.
     A. Nature of remark
         1. Classroom logistics: refers to the management of classroom activities such as homework assignments, roll, reading completed
         2. Reads or quotes from text
         3. Instructional statements: refers to the substantive issues under discussion
             If remarks were coded as instructional in focus, they were further analyzed for knowledge source and kind of reasoning.
             a. Knowledge source
                 (1) Personal-autobiographical (information drawn from the speaker's own experience)
                 (2) Text (information drawn from the text under study)
                 (3) Text-in-context (information about the author of the text, the historical period in which it was written, or its genre)
                 (4) General knowledge (information drawn from the media or contemporary culture that is widely available)
                 (5) Previous class discussions, lectures, or readings
                 (6) Other
             b. Kind of reasoning
                 (1) Summary-description (statements which focus on the literal features of an experience or text)
                 (2) Interpretation (statements which make an inference about the meaning or significance of information)
                 (3) Evaluation (statements that focus on the quality of an experience or a text)

      (4) Generalization (statements that move toward theoretical speculation about the nature of characters, authors, and texts)

      (5) Other

III. *Question:* any verbal or nonverbal gesture (as indicated in discussions that were videotaped) that invites or requires a response from an auditor

  A. Nature of question

    1. Classroom logistics

    2. Instructional focus

      If a question was coded as instructional, it was further analyzed for the knowledge source and level of reasoning it meant to elicit. Definitions for subcategories are the same as those for informational statements.

      a. Knowledge source

        (1) Personal-autobiographical

        (2) Text

        (3) Text-in-context

        (4) General knowledge

        (5) Previous class discussions-lectures-readings

        (6) Other

      b. Kind of reasoning

        (1) Summary-description

        (2) Interpretation

        (3) Evaluation

        (4) Generalization

        (5) Other

IV. *Respond:* any verbal or nonverbal gesture that acknowledges, restates, evaluates, or otherwise reacts to the nature, quality, or substance of preceding remarks. Responses clearly focus on the form or substance of the preceding remark itself. Answers to questions are coded in the "Inform" category. A remark coded as a response to a question would ask for a clarification or explanation of the question itself or would comment on the value of the question.

  A. Nature of response

    1. Acknowledgment (simple indication that a remark was heard)

    2. Restatement (an effort to repeat a previous remark)

    3. Positive evaluation (a positive comment on a previous remark)

    4. Negative evaluation (a negative comment on a previous remark)

    5. Request for explanation-elaboration-clarification (any remark that asks the previous speaker to speak more clearly or at greater length)

6. Elaboration upon a previous remark (any remark that moves beyond a simple restatement of a speaker's contribution by substantively changing the original speaker's language or by offering an interpretation of what the speaker is saying)
7. Other

V. *Other:* any utterance that cannot be coded within one of the four major categories

In all of our studies we used this basic coding scheme. We will detail the slight modifications Peter and Michael made when we present their chapters. But we first turn to Jim's studies on whole-class discussions of literature, for they provide the background against which to read the others.

3   Studies of Large-Group Discussions of Literature

Classroom discourse, like virtually any type of speech, represents what Bakhtin (1986) calls a "speech genre"; that is, the syntax, vocabulary, focus, tone, and other characteristics of spoken language that "signal a discourse community's norms, epistemology, ideology, and social ontology" (Berkenkotter & Huckin, 1993). All utterance, Bakhtin (1988) argues, is governed by some form of convention, whether we realize it or not. "Language," he says,

> is realized in the form of individual concrete utterances (oral and written) by participants in the various areas of human activity. These utterances reflect the specific conditions and goals of each such area not only through their content (thematic) and linguistic style, that is, the selection of the lexical, phraseological, and grammatical resources of the language, but above all through their compositional structure. All three of these aspects—thematic content, style, and compositional structure—are inseparably linked to the *whole* of the utterance and are equally determined by the specific nature of the particular sphere of communication. Each separate utterance is individual, of course, but each sphere in which language is used develops its own *relatively stable types* of utterances. These we may call *speech genres.* (p. 60)

In Bakhtin's (1986) view, all speech is shaped by genre, even though participants are often unaware of it. He argues that although "we use [speech genres] confidently and skillfully *in practice*, . . . it is quite possible for us not even to suspect their existence *in theory*" (p. 78). Our repertoire of genres is seemingly endless, and we switch from one (baby talk with an infant) to another (a discussion of dinner plans with a spouse) to another (a discussion of literature in an English class) effortlessly and often unconsciously.

Bakhtin's concept of speech genres is central to our discussion of classroom discourse, for the analysis of the teacher-led discussions that follows suggests that classroom discussions of literature share sufficient characteristics that they can usefully be understood as a speech genre. In this chapter we give conscious attention to the speech genre of literary discussions in order to understand its characteristics and its potential effects on the ways that students think about literature.

We wish to stress that we see speech genres as potentially flexible; we do not see them as having fatalistic implications for classroom discourse.

Mehan (1982) discusses the importance of recognizing "speech communities," which are

> defined through the shared or mutually complementary knowledge and
> abilities of its members for the production and interpretation of socially
> appropriate speech. Such a community is an "organization of diversity"
> (A. F. C. Wallace, quoted in Bauman and Sherzer 1974) insofar as this
> knowledge and ability is differentially distributed among its members;
> the production and interpretations of speech are thus variable and com-
> plementary, rather than homogeneous and constant, as grammatically
> based linguists have assumed. (p. 63)

Our account of the speech genre of classroom discussions of literature,
therefore, does not refer to a single, fixed way of talking, but rather to a genre
of discourse that, while including distinct characteristics, varies according to
the traits of the participants in particular situations.

Method

Participants

Sixteen teachers of English and their students participated in the study. The
teachers were selected on the basis of their experience and their reputation as
excellent instructors. Though all of them taught a variety of classes, for the
purposes of the research each was asked to select one class that primarily
involved the study of literature. The student participants were enrolled in the
classes chosen by the teachers. A smaller group of students (ranging from two
to seven from each class) provided case-study interviews. The upper-track and
lower-track classrooms studied were located in schools in the metropolitan
Albany area in New York. The middle-track classrooms were located in
schools in a suburban community in Iowa.

Data Collection

In the studies of upper-track and lower-track classrooms, eight teacher-researchers, themselves experienced teachers of literature, each studied one or
more teachers as those teachers taught an instructional unit on a literary text.
Before the study, the teacher-researchers had been active members of work-
shops sponsored by the National Writing Project and for at least a year had
participated in an ongoing seminar that focused on the relationships between
writing and literary understanding. The study reported here was in many ways
an outgrowth of questions raised by these practicing teachers as they reflected
together upon the nature and purposes of classroom discussions of literature.

In the study of middle-track classrooms, Mary Beth Hines, then a research fellow on the project, conducted interviews with seven teachers and a sample of their students and videotaped the classroom discussions.

Procedures

In order to examine the general patterns of discussion in these classrooms, each teacher's class was videotaped during all of the discussions of a single literary text. The videotapes were transcribed and later analyzed for their basic features. In order to explore teachers' and students' purposes during those discussions, each teacher and several students from each class were interviewed to determine their views of how discussions proceed and why they proceed as they do.

Interviews

The teachers were interviewed outside class, and while the specific questions in each interview varied depending on the text and the students being taught, all of the teachers were asked to address two basic issues: (1) What were their general purposes in holding discussion? and (2) What roles did they and their students typically play during discussions? The number of interviews with each teacher ranged from one to ten, depending on scheduling opportunities. The interviews were audiotaped and transcribed for later analysis.

Several students from each teacher's class were also interviewed for their perception of the purposes and patterns of classroom discussions. The number of students interviewed ranged from two to seven for each class (the seven students participated in a group interview), and the number of separate interviews ranged from one to four for each class, again depending on scheduling opportunities. These interviews were also audiotaped and transcribed for later analysis.

Videotaped Discussions

In an initial meeting with researchers, the participating teachers each decided upon the literary text that would be the focus of discussion during the videotaping. All of the texts selected were normally taught as part of the literature curriculum in the classes studied, and all of the teachers indicated that they would spend several consecutive days discussing them with their students.

On the days of the taping, a video camera was positioned as unobtrusively as possible in each room, and instruction proceeded as normally as possible. All of the teachers reported that the camera did not greatly affect their own or their students' participation in the discussions.

The number of classes videotaped ranged from three to five for each teacher, depending on the length of time the teacher devoted to the text under

Table 1

Summary of Data Collection for Large-Group Discussions

Teacher	Grade	Interviews		Observations	Text
		Teacher	Student		
Upper track					
K. Tucker	11/12	2	2	5	*Being There*
K. Phillips	11	3	1 (group)	4	*Ethan Frome*
G. Whitman	9	4	4	5	*Great Expectations*
F. Connelly	12	8	2	3	*Grapes of Wrath*
J. Allen	11/12	1	2	4	*Antigone*
C. Johnson	12	10	2	4	*I Heard the Owl Call My Name*
Middle track					
D. Stone	8	2	2	4	*When the Tripods Come*
K. Hadley	9	3	2	4	*The Pigman*
C. Anderson	10	4	4	4	*Hiroshima*
D. Overstreet	11	3	3	3	*Great Gatsby*
B. Kavale	12	3	2	4	*Death of a Salesman*
Lower track					
V. Carter	7	3	1	3	*Raymond's Run*
T. Carrera	10	11	1	4	*Law Like Love* *Book of the Grotesque*
J. Taggert	12	2	3	3	*Death of a Salesman*
L. Peters	10	5	written responses	3	*Of Mice and Men*
J. Vincent	8	2	1	3	*Mythology*
Totals		66	32	60	

study. In the end, sixty separate discussions of literature were transcribed and analyzed. The information about data collection is summarized in Table 1.

Transcriptions

The videotapes were viewed several times in the course of transcription in order to make certain that each speaker's contribution was accurately rendered. In a very few cases, students' contributions could not be heard in spite of repeated efforts to make them out. On these occasions, the student's turn was counted as one communication unit and was coded as "Other." Because such inaudible contributions may have sometimes been longer than one unit, the length of students' turns may be very slightly underrepresented in the analysis.

On most of the occasions when we had difficulty hearing students, however, we were helped by the teacher who very often repeated students' remarks, especially if those remarks were quietly spoken. We were able to reconstruct many otherwise inaudible contributions in this way.

Coding of Transcripts

The transcripts were coded according to the system outlined in Chapter 2. Two raters independently coded 15 randomly chosen transcripts of discussions, drawn equally from the three ability groups, representing 25 percent of the sample. Exact agreement between raters was 91 percent for the major categories and 86 percent for the subcategories.

Ability Grouping

Ability grouping is a central feature of life in many, if not most, American secondary schools, and our study of literature instruction could not escape that fact. Because many schools organize their curriculum around ability tracks, and because both teachers and students often view their work and themselves in terms shaped by ability grouping, we felt that an accurate portrait of instruction would need to include such grouping as an organizing principle. We intend no endorsement of tracking by structuring our study in this way, however. In fact, much of what we found in our research suggests the deeply problematic effects of such practices.

Teachers' and Students' Perspectives on Large-Group Discussions

All of the teachers and most of the students in these studies had had considerable experience with large-group discussions of literature. Over time and in a range of contexts, they had developed a set of expectations of how such discussions would proceed, an understanding of the roles teachers and students usually assumed, and some criteria that could be used to judge the success of the discussions that took place. In the sections that follow we explore the perspectives of teachers and students on large-group discussions on the basis of their responses to interview questions.

Teachers' Perspectives

Upper-Track Classrooms

The teachers working in upper-track classrooms seemed to proceed from a definition of discussion that emphasized the active participation of students. As Joe Allen put it:

> A classroom discussion, in my mind, is a class in which the students are reacting to the literature. They are either giving me some kind of feedback in terms of their understanding of the basic technical components or moving into a higher level application of the piece of literature to their own lives or to a deeper understanding of the piece.

The importance of students' reactions was echoed by Francis Connelly:

> It seems [to be] a question-and-answer period where—I'd never use a whole period for it—but where I start with questions and they respond. Then the responses start to jump around the room, where students are jumping in, sometimes without raising their hand, or just responding. Then the question-and-answer period has turned into a discussion period, and they move back and forth freely between the two. That technique is used a lot.

We should note that, though both of these teachers emphasize the centrality of students' responses, they also both speak of discussions in two parts: Allen speaks of students "giving feedback [on] . . . basic technical components" or "moving into a higher level application." Connelly suggests that his discussions begin with "a question-and-answer period" before "responses start to jump around the room, where students are jumping in, sometimes without raising their hand." While the goal is apparently to move toward the "higher applications" and away from "questions and answers," the teachers suggest that discussions have a structure that includes both kinds of thinking.

Karen Phillips also spoke of discussions as including a movement from one pattern of discourse to another. Asked to finish the phrase "A good classroom discussion is most like . . ." Phillips replied:

> I suppose I could . . . say it is most like a jam session. I'm not sure that is the right phrase, but you know what I mean. A good classroom discussion is most like an interaction of interested minds on a common topic.

But though the quality of discussions rests on the interaction of the participants, interaction alone is not enough. The purpose of discussions, she felt, is

> to get the class from their initial, personal responses and questions to the beginnings of an analysis or the beginnings of looking at ways that an

analysis can take place. I'm using . . . the discussion to lead them to find ways to get to a closer analysis of the text.

The goal of discussion for these teachers seems twofold. On the one hand, they would like to move their students toward a deeper and richer analysis of a text and away from "questions and answers" or the recapitulation of "technical components." At the same time, however, they would like to move the discussion toward the kinds of lively "interaction" described by Phillips and Allen. And the motives informing this goal are sometimes larger than simply wanting to improve students' understanding of literature. As Kevin Tucker put it:

> I think every kid should speak because I want to see them develop confidence in their ability to formulate their ideas verbally, to express those ideas to their peer group. . . . [When you don't speak] you have denied everybody else the opportunity of hearing your perspective, which is *your* perspective. . . . If there's a truth, it's only after hearing as many of the possible variations that may be present in this group. . . . It's a sort of duty to the group if you are going to have a discussion, it's a duty to the discussion. . . . There's something that you need to know that happens only when a kid contributes to a discussion.

If these teachers saw the nature and purpose of classroom discussion as twofold, they also saw a twofold role for themselves within those discussions. On the one hand, they saw themselves as "originators" (Connelly), "facilitators" (Grace Whitman), or "catalysts" (Tucker). Their role was to "get the topic started" (Connelly), "to see that everybody gets a chance to express himself or herself without . . . monopolizing the conversation" (Whitman), "to [keep] it going and [allow] everyone to get a chance who wants a chance" (Allen). In this view, the role of the teacher is to orchestrate the discussion almost invisibly. In fact, at times teachers stated as a kind of goal their own disappearance from the discussions. "If I do my job well in this course," Tucker argued, "by the time we reach the last major piece of fiction I shouldn't even have to be in the room." And Whitman suggested that a good classroom discussion would be "student centered . . . students' would be initiating the questions." Her own role would be simply to "watch it happen."

On the other hand, however, the teachers also recognized that their own role was central. As Phillips put it:

> Well, I'm more than a facilitator. I have structured activities so students have a place to begin. I'm very often a collector of their responses to begin with. . . . I usually ask a student to write down what's going on around us and, especially in the initial times of chaos—I am the person who makes sure we don't lose things and say, "Okay, everybody, be quiet Chris is going to say that again and Amy you make sure you get it down." Now that is just when we begin; then I guess I structure the process. We

get a whole bunch of ideas down and I say, "Okay Amy, would you go back through and read everything that we have collected and would the rest of you watch for what you think are patterns, what you think is more important than other things to lead our discussion to some kind of analysis."

The teachers saw part of their role, then, as organizing the potential "chaos" of discussion into coherence. As participants, they must make sure that "we don't lose things" and that the discussion leads to "some kind of analysis."

Teachers frequently said that they felt responsible for making certain the discussions "led" somewhere or "went" somewhere. As Carol Johnson put it:

I think the role of the teacher is to introduce some ideas that are maybe a springboard for some response. . . . However, I do feel sometimes when you feel the discussion is going a bit off track, then it's the responsibility of the teacher to get the students back on track a little bit and maybe that can be done through a simple summary of what's been said and what more has to be sort of explored or discussed.

Connelly echoed these thoughts when he suggested:

I'm serving to get the topic started. And then somewhat of a guide as the topic flows along, because if they move into what I consider total irrelevancies, then I would move them back.

The teachers saw their role, then, as more than one of maintaining order. Keeping the discussion "on track" and away from "irrelevancies" meant that teachers usually had a sense of what was to be covered in the course of the discussion. As Allen suggested:

I feel there are some important things I want students to see in a piece of literature. So I try to have that mix of their self-discovery of what's important and also the things I want them to find. And so occasionally I will become more the focus.

The teachers' sense of what students should "see" concerning the text under discussion often played an important part in the roles they saw for themselves. Tucker, for instance, articulated the general goals for his class this way:

I guess the ideal that I would like them to walk away with is a sense of how, through . . . within the last hundred years, from the late eighteen hundreds to the present time, significant writers have used the politics of human relationships to know that and feel comfortable with the notion that there . . . are no absolutes, which, for high school kids is very often a discomforting feeling rather than a comforting feeling.

Tucker wants his students, understandably, to leave his course with a particular body of knowledge. He wants them to have seen certain trends in the literature they have read, and to feel what he believes is a healthy discomfort about the themes that literature has explored. At the same time, however, as we saw earlier, he wants his students to "develop confidence in their ability to formulate ideas verbally, to express those ideas to their peer group." Like the other upper-track teachers, he has articulated a double purpose for discussions and a dual role for himself.

This theme of doubleness is perhaps the most central issue to emerge from the interviews with the upper-track teachers. On the one hand, teachers felt that they should facilitate discussions; on the other hand, they felt that they should make certain that the discussions "go somewhere." On the one hand, teachers tried to provide many students with the opportunity to speak; on the other hand, they felt that students should "see" certain things in the literature they read. On the one hand, discussions were "interactions"; on the other hand, the teachers often wanted to lead students further and deeper into an analysis of the text. Later in this chapter we will examine how these dual purposes were reflected in the patterns of talk during the discussions themselves. First, however, we will discuss the perspectives of teachers working in middle-track classrooms.

Middle-Track Classrooms

The teachers working with middle-track students also articulated a set of tensions informing their work, but in middle-track classrooms those tensions seemed to proceed less from conflicting purposes in orchestrating discussions than from the teachers' perception that their own goals in teaching literature were in conflict with their students' skills and motivation. Several of the teachers in this group began the interviews by outlining their larger purposes for teaching literature. Doug Overstreet, for instance, said that for him the study of literature is central to the entire educational mission:

> I'll begin by saying that I love literature myself and I'm biased—I think that everyone else should love it as much as I do. Of course, I'm not so idealistic as to believe that everybody will feel the same way. But I think that literature can be a great teacher, particularly in terms of learning about ourselves. I think literature does that better than anything else. Sometimes in my class I make fun of math, history, because I don't know if we learn that much about ourselves in such disciplines. . . . I think literature is the best at teaching.

Bea Kavale echoed Overstreet's observation that literature can teach students about themselves:

> I guess I want them to really think about how this fits into their lives. What ideas that the author is getting across can they use—can they find relevant in their lives. And maybe it won't make any difference to them now, but I hope, this is what I believe, I mean, this is what I kind of go on, that someday it, they'll remember this, and say, you know, I remem-

ber how these people dealt with the situation and now I can make a connection with that.

But literature can do more, according to these teachers, than help students understand themselves individually. It can also help them understand their connections to the larger world. It is a "body of knowledge" that they should share with others. Thus Carrie Anderson says:

I'm teaching in a democracy under a republican form of government and so when I set up goals for the students there are certain things, especially for literature, that I keep in mind. Number one goal is that I want them to have a common experience whether they're middle [track], top, or slow because I think you need a certain amount of conformity to make democracy work.

Kim Hadley repeats Anderson's theme and takes it one step further:

I think as a society there are certain types of literature that we have to have all experienced so that we have that as a society. . . . There are certain mores that society has, and I think those mores need to be covered in literature. If one of our tasks, and I believe it is one of our tasks, is to perpetuate the society in which we live, then I think we all need some common literature which speaks to those mores.

In the view of the teachers, then, literature itself should be a "teacher" that, on the one hand, helps students understand themselves as unique individuals and that, on the other, introduces them to the themes and values they will share with others in a democracy. It seems a noble conception of what literature is and what the teaching of literature is for, but it was balanced in the interviews by a less hopeful conception of who the average students were and what those students could do. Dan Stone, for instance, had this to say:

I think with the average-level student . . . one of the sources of the lack of motivation is the fact that many of them don't read well. If you don't do something well, you don't want to do it. Many of them have been read to in elementary school a lot, but I think one of the problems is very simple and I think it starts in the home. I do not think the parents have the children read. The kid comes home and he says "I'm going to do my work." Mom says fine. He goes up and turns on the TV set or the stereo and he works, but he really doesn't focus.

Kavale agreed with Stone's sense that average students were often distracted from their work:

They try to read in front of the TV or squish it in fifteen minutes here and think that they can read thirty-five pages and they zip through it so fast, that's a problem.

Anderson was more detailed in her analysis of the students. She told us:

> Second-trackers are made up of about three types. You have truly slow
> people who want to overachieve, like Bill. Have you spotted him yet?
> Glasses, second chair. And I do call on him and, as I said, he really needs
> extra help and he will come up to the lab when he gets stuck and he will
> come in and sit right next to me. . . . And then the second bunch that we
> have are people who are really, truly average and have ability, but they've
> never felt like really competing with anybody who is quite bright. And
> they're in here because they feel safe. . . . And then we have—that guy
> that just came back yesterday, Gentry. Gentry should be in top track. He
> can compete with anybody I've got in top track and that lazy son of a gun
> does not want to work. All he wants is a *C* in middle track and if he gets
> an *A* the next grade will come up an *F* so it averages out to a *C*. He's got
> this image and he is smart enough so that no matter what I do he's going
> to try and circumvent it so that's the game between us.

Anderson's perception of the three types of students found in the middle
track includes the range of students found by other teachers across the tracking system as a whole. In Anderson's view slow, average, and bright students
are all represented in the middle track—slow students because they try, bright
students because they don't, average students because they are average. When
teachers describe their students as having limited ability and motivation,
their task of teaching literature becomes a very challenging enterprise, especially since the teachers' articulated goals for their students are so broad and
optimistic.

How then do these teachers perceive their own classroom discussions?
Given their general goals in teaching literature, the individual teachers said
that they would like to orchestrate student-centered discussions in which their
own role would be minimal. But, given the traits of their students in the
middle track, all of the teachers felt that they had to take a much more central
role. As Stone put it:

> What I try to do in a classroom discussion is to involve as many students
> as I can. Basically they take two forms. Classroom discussions can be
> teacher-oriented or teacher-based or they can be student-based. Now
> [with the middle group] I can't do very much with student-based. There's
> just no way to do [it] because the clientele is not there. . . . You have to
> have leaders to have that student-based discussion.

Even with class leaders, though, the teachers often found it difficult to get
many of the students involved. Kavale described the problem for us:

> In the class you're going to see, sometimes it's harder to get them to
> contribute, and they will just as soon sit and listen and maybe not even
> listen at all and just, you know, I'm here but don't bother me. And so, I
> have to work at getting everybody involved whether they raise their hand
> or not, because not very many of them will raise their hand either. There
> are about, probably about five or six of the students that talk a lot. I mean
> they are more willing to, you know, discuss the story and who cares what

anybody else thinks. And then a lot of those kids in there will just sit back and let them do it unless I specifically call on them.

The five or six leaders in Kavale's class—the ones who will discuss the story and "who cares what anybody else thinks"—are apparently not enough to encourage their peers to speak up, and so Kavale, like Stone, finds that she must do a good deal of the work in keeping the discussion afloat.

The teachers suggested that, with average students, their own role in classroom discussions was almost always central, and they took various degrees of professional pride in that role. On the one hand, Anderson—the most experienced teacher in the group—had made her peace with the role of classroom leader. She told us:

> Having been through all the stages, truthfully, I am still teacher-centered. I guess because it works. My kids do well when they get away from me. And I get mail and they tell me what I didn't do well; they also tell me what was especially useful. When I try to do student-centered and it isn't structured, everything just goes to pot. I don't have that knack. I figure they'll get that from somebody else. It's not my style.

But even those teachers from whom students might "get" the student-centered approach seem to be struggling to make it work. Overstreet, only in his second year of teaching, had this to say:

> The class is discussion-based. The students do the talking about the literature. . . . The problem that I've noticed so far is that I'm doing a lot more talking than I wish I had to. I wish that I could do less and let the students do more. And there are a variety of reasons for that. Some unavoidable things such as the fact that the class is large and that it's the first class in the morning. [But] that's kind of like putting the blame somewhere else. "Well, it's the first period class, they don't talk, it's not my fault, they're still sleeping" or something like that. But I don't think that's the main reason. Part of it lies in myself. I know for example, this book, *The Great Gatsby,* I'm trying to decide how much I need to teach from the book. Do I have to point out every little detail? I feel compelled to do so—I seem to be pointing things out to them all the time. And maybe what I'm waiting for is idealistically for some student to say, "Mr. Overstreet, did you see that line on page 127? What a great line! I think that he was trying to say—" Et cetera, et cetera. And instead, I'm leading them to conclusions that I have already formulated, I think. I think that might be what I'm doing rather than allowing them to formulate their own conclusions.

The teachers' ambivalence about their own roles in the discussions underscores the theme of doubleness that characterized the interviews. The teachers seemed caught between what they felt they needed to do to engage the students, and what they felt they had to do to arrive at a responsible reading of the story. The teachers *wanted* the students to be able to determine their own conclusions, and when the students didn't or couldn't, they felt compelled to lead them towards a "proper" reading of the literature. Teachers were troubled by this doubleness to varying degrees. Some, like Anderson, felt comfortable with their role as authoritative leader; others, like Overstreet, seemed conflicted about the inconsistency between their ideals and their practice.

We will see more clearly how these teachers led discussions and formulated conclusions when we examine the language of the discussions. First, though, we will examine the perspectives of teachers working in lower-track classrooms.

Lower-Track Classrooms

The teachers working in lower-track classrooms faced an entirely different set of challenges than did those working with upper-track or even middle-track students. The lower-track classrooms were populated by students with histories of school frustration and failure—students who rarely spoke of further education and who seemed to show little interest in addressing the standard, academic approaches to literature. The teachers here, then, articulated a third kind of tension: a conflict between their own goal of engaging students with literature on a personal level and their students' unwillingness to engage with any material delivered, however skillfully, through the school curriculum.

Of all the teachers interviewed, those working with lower-track students were most consistent in stating their hope that students would engage with literature on a personal level, would construct a meaning that made sense to them. As Jean Taggert put it:

> I really try to find out what they think. This is the interesting part, the most complicated, the most meaningful. What within the [text] affects your own life?

The centrality of students' active participation in the process of interpretation was echoed by Tony Carrera:

> I want students to be able to make [literature], both as readers and writers. I want them to be independent interpreters. If interpretation, if one level of it is going to be personal, then I want it to start there. I want it to start as being personal. I would like some individual engagement first, with the opportunity, at least for a couple of minutes, to think about, what have I got here? What am I doing? [Discussions] are a group of people deciding what they need to build, building it, and then deciding whether it's any good or not.

The specific purposes informing discussions of literature were in large measure the same as those informing the teachers' general purposes in teaching. As Veronica Carter argued:

> I see as my purpose in the classroom to keep going a feeling that we are people, first of all, and we are educating ourselves. We're learning things together about the text, about each other, about what we think about the world, and it's more than . . . I'm in here educating people and our finished product is people that I have finished molding somehow. They're not going to be finished any more than I'm finished now. You don't send people out of high school knowing everything they need to know. You send them out eager to learn.

What perhaps seems most striking about these excerpts from the interviews is the articulate passion with which the teachers were able to describe their goals. Less obvious, though perhaps equally important, is the fact that these teachers seldom set for themselves the goal of leading students toward an understanding of conventional textual meaning or the appreciation of authorial intention. Their interest, rather, seemed focused on the ways texts could be used to foster students' reflection on their lives, their peers, their communities. In this view, the understanding of literary texts is not an end of instruction, but the means by which students are led to a richer and more fully developed understanding of themselves.

A convenient label for such goals might be "student-centered" or "reader-centered" (as opposed to "teacher-centered" or "text-centered"), but such a label would greatly simplify and thus seriously misrepresent the difficulties these teachers faced in achieving their goals. For though they hoped that their students would read and discuss texts in ways that were meaningful to them, they sought to accomplish that task with students who were not accustomed to such discussions and within an instructional context that provided little support for their efforts.

By definition, the students enrolled in the classes studied here were generally not college bound. They had been designated as average ability or lower, possessed of problems in reading comprehension, writing ability, and various "school skills" such as attentiveness, regular attendance, and appropriate behavior in class. The teachers working with these students usually could not assume even the most basic comprehension of what had been read. Hence, though her goal was always to find out what her students thought about a text, Taggert suggested that she must first ask:

> Just on this literal level, did they understand what happened? After we've read it, we want to go back over it. Do they really know what happened? Are they confused by the flashbacks? Are they confused by the mix-up of characters? Very basically, have [they] truly comprehended this work and [do they] know what happened? Then I really try to find out what they think.

The students' problems with comprehension, of course, make it difficult for Taggert to get them to read at all:

I did have them read, and I don't know if that was a mistake. It's such a battle. You have absolutely no idea. The anger. The resistance. They have never been asked to read before out of the room, and that is the truth. They can't believe that I am expecting them to read this story by themselves. . . . The [stories] that I know are tough, I start it and set up the characters. I get names on the board so they're not confused, and the setting, where it takes place, and I move as far as them reading aloud. I read some myself, asking some to read who are willing to do that, who are good readers. We establish what I consider security information so that people are not so intimidated. [But] they read the two opening paragraphs and they are lost. They are not readers and they are tired. And they are annoyed that they are being asked to read at all.

Here it seems clear that Taggert's student-centered desire to help her students think personally about the text ("What within the text affects your own life?") can be achieved only when that thinking is preceded by teacher-centered strategies (reading aloud, putting names on the board, establishing the setting, providing "security information"). In her plans for a discussion of *Of Mice and Men,* Laura Peters took similar precautions:

I'm going to introduce the characters of George and Lennie. I think I'm going to have them work on George to get down details of George and Lennie. The description passage I may type up and let them work in partners and let them underline concrete words and that kind of thing. [The only difficulty I see] is if they haven't read it. But even now they might be able to get through the class, the way the class is set up [with the typed description provided].

The problems that these teachers described in helping their students "through class" and to a simple comprehension of what the texts say, however, were compounded by students' attitudes toward the language and conventions of schooling itself. As Taggert put it:

One of the interesting things I've found is that they are so afraid of arguing. They call it "arguing," "fighting." It makes some of them very uncomfortable. I call it a wonderful discussion. You say something. I counter. You come back. I counter. Document your opinion. Keep at me. [But they don't do that.] I don't think they have enough practice. How many homes allow that kind of [discussion]? Encourage it? The mere intellectual exercise of it all isn't something they value. They don't have an investment in discussion unless there is something concrete like they are going to get out of something, or they are going to get something raised.

That at least some of Taggert's students cannot perceive argument as a kind of "intellectual exercise" is a reminder that students may have difficulty with a curriculum not only because of its content, but also because of its form. The modes of argumentation that are taken for granted in school, and in most academic discourse, may themselves be an obstacle, Taggert suggested, to her students' participation in the literate community she represents and into which she is trying to invite them.

That literate community, though, is forged largely in schools, and while the characteristics of their students pose one challenge for teachers, the characteristics of schooling pose another that may be equally difficult to overcome. One of the problems, as Carrera suggested, is that schools seem to place a greater value on right answers than on careful thinking:

> One of the things I think people have been trained to do . . . is come up with a fill-in-the-blank answer and that's it. It's either right or wrong, and there's no sense going any further with it because nobody cares. And I don't think anybody can read a work or live a life that way and there seems to be a lot of training that goes on in school that tells you, setting this problem, yes or no, and then write one sentence that gives yes or no and then stop. Don't worry about it, don't ever try to fashion that into a whole interpretation of the work.

The emphasis on fill-in-the-blank answers, however, by providing few occasions for students to engage in extended thought, works to undermine the efforts of teachers who may want to help students move beyond such answers. Thus Peters, following the class in which students worked in groups on Steinbeck's characterization of George and Lennie, had this to say:

> It was awful. It was terrible. I was really not happy with it. I know I didn't accomplish what I wanted to accomplish. The kids didn't seem to know what it was I was asking them to do. And the kids had a problem speaking. I asked for individuals to get up and speak, to represent these groups and they had a problem with that. [And] when I tried to pull it all together it was a real disaster. [So, tomorrow] I'm going to be in charge, control more of the classroom. Maybe it will be better, they'll know what they're talking about tomorrow. But I don't know.

The problem is circular. Students are given little practice in independent discussion, and so, when they are asked to participate in a small or large group, they have limited command of the conventions and achieve limited success. In Bakhtin's terms (1986; see also Wertsch, 1991), the students have not had the opportunity to participate in the speech genre for discussing literature in the school setting. Their teachers, meanwhile, frustrated at the disarray of the discussion and disappointed that their own goals have not been met, are pushed back in the very direction they were hoping to avoid. Thus Peters, having decided to be "more in charge" in her teaching of *Of Mice and Men,* said she was happy after the second day of discussion:

> I got the kids to go in the direction I wanted to. I think the class was more teacher-directed. I felt the kids were all with me and knew what I was talking about and read what I asked them to read. And finished things the way I wanted to.

At times, in spite of the pressure to locate "right answers" and in spite of students' reluctance to enter fully into a discussion, these teachers felt success. After one such class, Carter said:

> I was exactly where I wanted to be in the classroom for almost all of that class. I felt like I was in a community of people who were interested in what I was interested in and I felt like I was taking part in a literary discussion. They said some things that were interesting to me personally as a reader that I want to use in informing my own reading of the work. They did not act like little vessels ready to be filled with facts at all.

Given the characteristics of their students and the characteristics of schooling, however, such discussions were unfortunately only rarely achieved.

Summary

Teachers working within each of the ability levels we studied articulated a set of conflicts or tensions that helped shape the discussions that took place in their classrooms. Teachers working with upper-track students saw a tension between their desire to facilitate discussions in which students explored texts on their own terms and the need to make certain that that discussion led to a clearly articulated interpretation of the text. Teachers working with middle-track students, on the other hand, saw a conflict between their own purposes in reading and teaching literature and their students' motivation and skill in pursuing those purposes. And teachers working with lower-track students saw a conflict between their goal of helping students engage personally with literature and their students' unwillingness to so engage. Though the source of these tensions in each case was different, the result, in the teachers' reports, was the same: a move away from the student-centered discussions the teachers saw as ideal toward the teacher-dominated discussions that most hoped to avoid. Later in this chapter we will examine how the tensions perceived by these teachers affected the discussions themselves. But first we will describe the students' own perspectives on discussions of literature.

Students' Perspectives

Upper-Track Classrooms

In large measure, the students we interviewed across ability levels described the purposes of discussion and the roles of teacher and student during discussions in much the same way their teachers did. Lucy, for instance, an upper-track student in Francis Connelly's classroom, defined discussions this way:

> I think, um, usually it's the interaction between students and it's also interaction with the teacher. It might be, like just . . . he'll want to know what our feelings are on something. Like the symbolism in *The*

> *Grapes of Wrath* or . . . and the people put forth their opinions and their
> ideas. . . . Usually it's more like people contributing their ideas . . . their
> opinions and things like that.

Lucy described the teacher's role as "initiator":

> He would like say something and ask the class what they feel about it.
> And he would ask us for our opinion, ask us for our ideas, and he might
> be like an instigator . . . keep it going, keep the discussion going, and like
> pursue what we're trying to say. If we're saying something he would like
> try to go into it deeper.

The purpose of the discussion, from Lucy's perspective, seems clear:

> To promote critical thinking and to follow through with some kind of
> lesson he has prepared. Or just to find out what we're thinking, and get
> us to start using our logic and brain power and knowledge a little bit.

But though teachers are "initiators" of discussion, they are also, in the
students' view, guides who lead students through the text. Mary, a student in
Carol Johnson's class, suggested that Johnson

> is the leader. She's leader of the group and every group needs a leader.
> . . . I don't think we would just come in and start talking about important
> parts of the text. She's an expert at this because she's read the text several
> times and studied it several times and she knows what parts she thinks
> are important and we would all have conflicting ideas of what would be
> important if it weren't for her because she keeps us on track.

If the teacher's role is to initiate the discussion and then keep the students "on
track," the students saw their own role as one of thoughtful participation. Sam,
an upper-track student in Joe Allen's class, described his contributions this
way:

> I listen to others' opinions. Hear what's happening, and then if I disagree
> or have some questions about something, I will ask. That's basically what
> I do. I try to listen and see what's going on. See what people think. And
> then I try to relate that to what I think [is] going on. And if I have any
> questions, I'll ask.

Several students said that they tried to make certain that their contributions
would be useful and relevant to the unfolding discussions. Mary, for example,
said:

> I keep quiet unless I think I have something really important to say. I
> think when I do say things . . . they are well thought out because I don't
> just talk the whole time. I really think about it and if I say something, I
> think I usually say it because I think it's something important, . . . some-
> thing that no one else has thought of. If I think of something that I think
> other people probably have thought of, I don't usually say it.

The upper-track students, in other words, often felt a responsibility to *stay* "on track," just as their teachers felt a responsibility to keep them there. Their contributions to the discussions were not, they felt, random or repetitive. They believed their comments were relevant to what had already been said, woven into the talk in a way that would be helpful to the other students in class.

The upper-track students, like their teachers, then, saw discussions as occasions for the lively exchange of ideas, but also as interactions directed toward particular ends. They felt they had a responsibility to share their views, but they also felt that those views should be expressed in a coherent and helpful way.

Middle-Track Classrooms

Students in middle-track classrooms viewed discussions differently than did their upper-track peers. But like their peers, middle-track students shared the perspective of their teachers.

If the middle-track teachers felt that their own role in discussions was to guide, lead, and often inform, the students felt that their own role was to listen and become informed. Rarely, in fact, did students mention their own participation. Edward, for instance, from Dan Stone's class, answered this way when he was asked about his role in discussion:

> Listening most of the time to get all of the information we can of what he's talking about. . . . Basically what happens is he'll have us go home and read the chapter over and we just [go] over the big information we need to know for like quizzes and tests, that type of thing.

Melanie, from Carrie Anderson's class, had a comparable perspective on her role in discussions:

> Just to absorb what she's saying and to, you know, if you have a question about something, ask it, or else, you know, you won't know it.

The teacher's role, according to Melanie, is equally direct:

> To make sure that we know the information well and make sure, I mean, you know, go over the book and make sure we're prepared.

When the teachers tried to do more than simply provide information, the students sometimes expressed frustration. Abbey, from Doug Overstreet's class, had this to say about his discussion of *Gatsby:*

> He talks about the book and the characters and I think we spend too much time. I think we took too long on *The Great Gatsby.* . . . It was not that long of a book and it's not that hard to read. . . . Some of the things, it's almost irrelevant to say them because everyone should know it. Like about in the book that Tom is an overbearing character. Well, you get that

in the first chapter. You know that, you know, it's not something that needs to be discussed, I don't feel.

There seems to be an emphasis on efficiency in the students' reports—a sense that teachers and students have designated roles, that there is an exchange of information to be conducted, and that the best classes are ones in which these things are done quickly and directly.

Don, a senior from Bea Kavale's class, gave us the clearest perspective on why middle-track students may bring such attitudes to their literature classrooms. For most of his high school career, Don had been an upper-track student in English class. He told us why he had "dropped down" to the middle track in his last year:

> It was my senior year and I really wanted to slow down my pace and I'm in more activities than just inside school. I do a lot of things after school and I didn't feel I needed to take a top track. I didn't want to be doing research all the time.

When asked about the differences between the top and middle tracks, Don was very direct:

> The kids are more stimulating in the top track and more interested in the group activities versus the kids in the middle track. Middle-track kids kind of whine and cry and they're kind of babies actually.

Middle-track discussions, from Don's perspective, were exactly as the teachers have described them:

> Usually Ms. Kavale does the majority of talking because, and this is just my opinion, a lot of the kids in here don't like to work. A lot of them aren't that smart and they don't come up with questions. She always comes up with questions, makes us go digging for it. [In the upper track], it hasn't been that way. [There], we discuss what we want to discuss. Ms. Kavale leads us through. She decides what we're going to talk about because I don't think the majority of the kids could actually lead a discussion.

But when he was asked why middle-track students may have such difficulties, Don was able to take a broader view:

> I think at a young age we were separated into the smart people, the regular, and the dumb. And the smart people, everybody knew, were above everyone else and they were expected to work, and they were going to learn. The middle kids said, "Ah, forget it, we don't care, we'll get through high school." They didn't push themselves. And the dumb kids, they still get help and they are pushed, and eventually could probably become smarter than the middle-track people. They might not do as much material as the middle-track people, but the material they do they will understand better. . . . In the middle track, Ms. Kavale doesn't push

it like in the lower track and the top track. Not to say that she's a bad teacher for it. She does what she can, but she knows that these kids are not interested for one, and they don't want to continue on. Whereas I think that the lower-track kids, they do want to learn but they don't understand. The top-track kids do want to learn and they do understand.

In Don's analysis, then, middle-track students are taught to "forget it," to just "get through"—and they learn the lesson well. By the time they reach the twelfth grade, the average students have learned to expect neither the extra help lower-track students receive nor the academic challenges provided for students in the upper tracks. Instead, they get by, causing few problems, raising few questions, "listening for the information" they might need for the next quiz.

Lower-Track Classrooms

Like their peers in the other ability tracks, the students we interviewed from lower-track classrooms saw the goals and problems of discussions in much the same way their teachers did. Several students suggested that those goals included the opportunity for them to learn more about themselves. As Julie, a student in Tony Carrera's class, put it:

> [A discussion is] just telling our own ideas about any work, just about anything. We try to get on one topic and discuss that which will lead us to other topics. The interpretation will help you try to understand meanings about a work or a lot of times it's just to see, to learn more about yourself. Interpretation is mainly what does it because you learn about yourself in a way—how you feel about the use of certain words, how you feel about a certain topic that the author has thought about, and if you agree or disagree with them. 'Cause that's what makes the world go around—there's agreements and disagreements.

The theme of openness to students' ideas was echoed by Jessica, a student in Veronica Carter's class:

> [Carter] wants us to figure things out for ourselves. So maybe even though she's sorted some things out in her head, she's open about our ideas. And she's interested to see whether we can figure things out. She wants us to try to be able to figure things out by ourselves, even though it's not the same way she interpreted the text, she says that it's not necessarily wrong.

But if openness and the free play of ideas are the goal of discussion, some of the students recognized that their teachers played a significant role in guiding and controlling the conversation. Tony, for example, a student in Jim Vincent's class, described discussions this way:

We have discussions all the time. Like what did you think was most important, what do you think you learned, what did you get out of that, what did this mean, what happened with this, what happened with that, and what do you think will happen later and stuff like that.

To answer such questions, however, Tony needs the help of his teacher:

He's going to tell us the story because he said the reading would be too hard. He reads the book and he puts it into his own words because he doesn't think we could understand the book.

Retelling the story for students (in this case, stories from mythology) makes it possible for students to begin the interpretive process embodied in Vincent's questions ("What do you think you learned? What do you think will happen later?"). But the teacher here is clearly making an enormous effort to support that process, providing the kind of "security information" that Laura Peters mentioned. The problem becomes how to provide such security without undermining the student-centered interpretive practice that it is meant to serve. The students in these classes seemed to need support from their teachers in their efforts to read literature. Their alienation from school, and from the orderly, middle-class values represented by school, is often profound. David, a student in Jean Taggert's twelfth-grade class, put it this way:

A lot of [teachers] think they know everything. They tell people, "Well, when you get out in the real world. . . ." They really don't know nothing about the real world. They try to tell us, "When you get out there, go to work and be there on time." You know, all kind of stuff like that. When kids go out and do that, they are going to get fucked over, you know. Teachers here are trying to have kids go by the rules and play everything straight. When you go out, everything isn't straight, man. It's a dog-eat-dog world. That's the way I look at it. That's how things have been for me.

David feels separated, though, not just from the world of school, but also from the people in school who make the rules and seem to succeed:

Like we got sides in this school. The scumbags and the higher people. People look at you, just 'cause you got a leather jacket or you got your head shaved or you got long hair, got Doc Martin boots or holes in your pants, people look at you like you're scumbags. You ain't got no polo shirt on, you know? Gold around your neck, driving a BMW to school. You're garbage.

David's representation of his life, both in and out of school, perhaps needs little commentary. But given that representation, we can already see the difficulties his teacher would face in sustaining a discussion about literature that would not only include him, but would also seek out and support his efforts to connect the literature to what he knows. For what he knows is different from what other, more academically successful students might know—and David realizes how different that knowledge is:

> 'Cause we have a totally different life, the way we live. We just don't have a life where we wake up in the morning, go to school, do our schoolwork and then go home, do our homework and then we go to bed or eat dinner with our Mommy and Daddy, you know. We don't have a life like that.

The teachers we studied attempted to discuss literature in ways that would help students like David see their lives and their communities more clearly. But as David pointed out so forcefully, the deeper problem may be that schools do not see students as clearly as they might.

Summary

The expectations and attitudes that teachers and students bring to classroom discussions will of course help shape the kinds of discussions that take place. Yet what seems most striking about these interviews is how deeply students and teachers appear to share an understanding of the roles each should play in classroom discussions. Students seem to assume the roles they have been given, to see themselves largely as they have been seen, and to internalize the tensions that their teachers have articulated. We next turn our attention to how those tensions inform the discussions themselves.

The Language of Large-Group Discussions of Literature

The striking similarities between the teachers' and students' understanding of the roles they play in large-group discussions of literature suggest that these discussions can be regarded as a speech genre, a form of talk where "certain patterns of speaking and thinking are easier, or come to be viewed as more appropriate . . . than others" (Wertsch, 1991, p. 38). In the following analysis, we explore in greater depth the patterns of speaking and thinking that characterized teacher-led discussions of literature. By examining the ways in which teachers and students speak during discussions, we hope to see more clearly the manner in which students are encouraged to participate in literature classrooms, and the type of thinking promoted through the manner of their participation.

Speaker Turns

The patterns of turn-taking among teachers and students during the classes observed were comparable in most respects to those reported in earlier studies

Table 2

Mean Number of Turns by Speaker

	Teacher	*SD*	Students	*SD*
Upper track (*n* = 2,769)	60.7	52.8	70.4	55.1
Middle track (*n* = 4,979)	111.4	34.7	150.4	63.0
Lower track (*n* = 1,687)	56.5	19.8	61.3	21.9
Average (*N* = 9,435)	86.7	30.5	111.0	49.0

of classroom discourse (Sinclair & Coulthard, 1975; Mehan, 1979; Cazden, 1988). As Table 2 indicates, the turns here were distributed fairly evenly among teachers and students within ability groups if students are considered as a group. The average number of turns taken by teachers during discussion ranged from 56.5 to 111.4, with a mean of 86.7. The average number of turns taken by students meanwhile ranged from 61.3 to 150.4, with a mean of 111. The generally even distribution of turns among teachers and students across ability groups suggests that in most discussions the floor was returned to the teacher after each student contribution. In those classes where students' turns outnumbered the teacher's turns, students averaged slightly more than one turn for each turn taken by the teacher.

A more telling indication of teachers' and students' relative contributions to discussions is provided by the average number of communication units per participant turn; that is, the number of statements coded within each turn. As summarized in Table 3, teachers averaged from 3.7 to 6.5 communication units per turn, with a mean of 5.4, while students averaged from 1.4 to 2.1 communication units per turn, with a mean of 1.8. In general, teachers' turns were about two to five times longer than students' turns.

We can see one example of these patterns in an excerpt from Kevin Tucker's upper-track class discussion of Jerzy Kosinski's *Being There*. Tucker began the class by reminding the students of what they had discussed the day before. On that day he wanted to make a transition to a discussion of the institutions with which Kosinski deals in his novel, but before doing so he asked the students to take a close look at the first paragraph of the novel:

> *Tucker:* Now, I just want to take one additional look before I make the transition here to the institutions that Kosinski deals with. To, if you will allow me, the very first page, all right? I'm glad no one said, "No, I won't allow you." You're very polite. [I often put emphasis] on beginnings and endings, the first paragraph of a short story, the beginning, the first line of a poem. I'm a Poe-ist in that regard, Edgar Allan Poe's theory about the significance of every word, every line in a short story. The significance of a first line, that it should not be wasted. You don't have that kind of time. And here, rather than just toss this off, not only does the first

Table 3

Mean Number of Communication Units within Turns by Speaker

	Teacher	SD	Students	SD
Upper track (n = 2,769)	3.7	5.0	1.4	1.0
Middle track (n = 4,979)	6.0	15.2	2.1	1.3
Lower track (n = 1,687)	6.5	6.7	1.7	0.4
Average (N = 9,435)	5.4	1.5	1.8	2.2

paragraph often serve to give some kind of focus, but then we end up with another literary technique here. When writers start throwing similes and metaphors at you, boom! Indication! Alert time! You know, he's taking the time to make some form of comparison, either direct or indirect, whatever the case may be. What's he doing in paragraph one?

Student: [inaudible] Comparing people to plants.

Tucker: Comparing people to plants. Okay. Using what technique?

Student: Simile.

Tucker: Simile. Okay. There's that key word "like" in there. [reads from text] Okay, in that regard, plants are like people. Are there more, perhaps some ways in which plants are not like people?

Student: They don't have feelings.

Tucker: No feelings. Interesting simile, but to what extent does the simile actually apply? He's given us three specific criterion here. . . .

We will be looking more closely at the qualitative differences between teachers' and students' contributions to discussion in the section that follows, but for the present this excerpt may suggest the strong quantitative differences in those contributions. Tucker speaks more frequently than any individual student; the floor is returned to him after each student's turn. More important, perhaps, his turns are significantly longer than students' turns. Students offer only a sentence, sometimes only a single word, in their turns, while Tucker typically repeats and then elaborates upon what students have said, adding detail and raising related questions. We will turn now to examine more specifically the language and content of participants' contributions to classroom discussion.

General Patterns in the Discussions

As we explain in Chapter 2, each communication unit was coded within one of four major categories: "Direct," "Inform," "Question," and "Respond." A fifth category, "Other," included all remarks that could not be coded within major categories. The relevant data for teachers and students are summarized in Table 4.

Table 4

General Discourse Functions:
Percentage of Communication Units across Turns

	n of Units	Direct	Inform	Question	Respond	Other
Upper track						
Teacher	4,759	11.1	48.0	22.7	18.0	0.1
Student	1,992	0	86.0	13.2	0.1	0.1
Middle track						
Teacher	7,747	1.7	66.8	20.0	11.5	0
Student	3,185	0.1	78.3	16.4	4.8	0
Lower track						
Teacher	5,380	2.1	63.9	22.5	11.1	0.3
Student	1,604	0	76.4	11.7	4.5	6.9
Total						
Teacher	17,886	4.3 (3.1)	60.9 (10.1)	21.4 (1.5)	13.1 (3.8)	0.1 (0)
Student	6,781	0 (0)	80.1 (5.1)	14.3 (2.4)	3.3 (2.6)	1.6 (3.9)

Note: Numbers in parentheses are standard deviations.

As indicated in the table, there were on the average strong differences in the proportion of remarks made by teachers and students within each of the major categories. Across sixty classroom discussions, fewer than 1 percent of students' remarks were coded as directive in function, while 4.3 percent of teachers' remarks were so coded. Meanwhile, 80.1 percent of students' remarks were informative, while only 60.9 percent of the teachers' remarks were intended to inform. In general, teachers were more likely than their students to ask questions when speaking (21.4 percent for teachers, 14.3 percent for students) and were much more likely than their students to respond to a previous contribution (13.1 percent for teachers, and 3.3 percent for students). Less than 2 percent of teachers' and students' contributions were coded as "Other."

On the average, then, teachers' remarks ranged rather widely across the four language functions, while students' remarks were most frequently informative in purpose. We can see these patterns from a slightly different perspective by examining the proportions of functions served within speakers' turns. The relevant information for teachers and students is summarized in Table 5.

Across ability groups the teachers were likely, within any given turn, to respond to a previous remark (23.9 percent), make an informative statement (44.6 percent), and ask a question (28.1 percent). These three functions seem to constitute a basic three-part structure of teachers' turns during discussions.

Table 5

General Discourse Function:
Percentage of Communication Units within Turns

	n of Units	Direct	Inform	Question	Respond	Other
Upper track	6,751					
Teacher		6.5	32.2	27.3	34.0	0.1
		(19.0)	(38.4)	(35.0)	(40.9)	(2.0)
Student		0	84.1	14.7	1.2	0.1
		(0)	(35.8)	(34.6)	(10.6)	(2.7)
Middle track	10,932					
Teacher		1.4	48.8	28.4	21.0	0
		(1.6)	(9.6)	(3.5)	(5.7)	(0)
Student		0.1	79.4	15.3	5.2	0
		(0.1)	(11.9)	(8.2)	(5.8)	(0)
Lower track	6,984					
Teacher		1.8	50.2	28.6	18.8	0.2
		(1.6)	(20.0)	(9.9)	(11.3)	(0.3)
Student		0	71.2	11.3	3.9	13.3
		(0)	(12.6)	(6.1)	(4.1)	(11.4)
Average	24,667					
Teacher		2.9	44.6	28.1	23.9	0.1
		(2.8)	(10.0)	(0.7)	(8.2)	(0)
Student		0	78.4	14.0	3.7	3.8
		(0)	(6.5)	(2.1)	(2.0)	(7.6)

Note: Numbers in parentheses are standard deviations.

But these averages mask some important differences among the ability groups. Among teachers working with upper-track students, informative statements make up about a third of the teachers' turns, while among those working with middle- and lower-track students such statements constitute on average fully half of the teachers' turns. Moreover, teachers in upper-track classrooms respond to their students' contributions almost twice as often as did teachers working at the other levels.

Students' turns, across the ability levels, were dominated by an informative purpose: 78.4 percent of their remarks within turns were informative, with most of the remainder devoted to asking questions (14 percent). This pattern is consonant with the relative brevity of students' turns (just over one remark per turn). When they held the floor, students were most likely to make a single informative remark or ask a single question.

We can see an example of these various patterns in excerpts from two discussions. The first is from Carol Johnson's discussion of Margaret Craven's *I Heard the Owl Call My Name* in an upper-track classroom. For homework, students had generated a list of images from the novel that they found especially powerful. Johnson begins the discussion by asking students to describe those images.

> *Johnson:* Okay, well, we're here to talk about death and life, I suppose, in other ways and other terms, but through Margaret Craven and her voice, and, but we want to play a little bit first, we really want to use some of the images that you generated in your lists last night. So let's begin with those. What are the most powerful images for you in the work and we are—I'm hoping to help you begin to construct a final paper for this work and so that we will be concluded with it by Friday and move on to *Ironweed* next week, but that's what we're really doing today and we will continue to do a little bit of this on Friday as well in maybe a more structured way on Friday, but give me some of the images that are most vivid for you from this work.
>
> *Student:* The eyes.
>
> *Johnson:* The eyes, okay. [writes on board]
>
> *Student:* I thought all the elements of nature were really important, but like animals and the foliage and things like that.
>
> *Student:* Water.
>
> *Johnson:* All right, let's be specific because it will help in the long run. Okay, water. The animals, which ones?
>
> *Student:* The owl. The fish.
>
> *Student:* They also talked about the killer whale.
>
> *Johnson:* The killer whale.
>
> *Student:* The wolf.
>
> *Student:* The bear.
>
> *Johnson:* Okay, I'm going to ask you to recall—remember the myths that are attached to those, okay? Maybe we'll go back to those and just, in a short while, but—okay, some other images.
>
> *Student:* Seasons.
>
> *Student:* Colors.
>
> *Student:* Mashed turnips.
>
> *Johnson:* I hadn't thought about that, it seems to be such a little minor detail, but it's interesting, we can use it. Okay, I missed something someone said, religion.
>
> *Student:* [inaudible]
>
> *Johnson:* What was connected with, if religion and ritual go hand in hand in your mind, given particular scenes in the story, what objects symbolized their ritual?
>
> *Student:* Holding the lamb.
>
> *Johnson:* Holding the lamb?

Student: Christ.

Johnson: Okay, I couldn't remember that. The masks. The picture you're referring to really, aren't you? Christ was depicted as holding the lamb, the eyes if I'm remembering correctly from the very beginning of the book. Okay, anything else?

Student: [inaudible] eagle on it.

Johnson: All right, again, I think all of these perhaps, the objects in the church maybe let's say. Okay, that's good. Now would someone do me a favor, please, and copy these down in a list for me so that I can take it away from class today. . . .

The purpose of this activity is to generate a list of images, to brainstorm, to get a set of issues on the floor for later discussion. Thus the abbreviated turns taken by students are understandable. But if we consider the excerpt as a whole, we can ask what purposes were served by the contributions of Johnson and her students.

It seems clear that Johnson has provided the context in which the remarks of the students will be meaningful. Almost all of the students' contributions consist of incomplete sentences, nouns without predicates, that can be understood only within the framework that the teacher has constructed. By the very nature of the activity, students are under little obligation to elaborate upon their contributions or to reason further about them. They need only to make their suggestions in the form of informative statements. The teacher weaves the disparate elements into coherent discourse ("if religion and ritual go hand in hand . . . what objects symbolized their ritual?"), provides background information ("The masks. The picture you're referring to really, aren't you?"), and sets the stage for further discussion ("I'm going to ask you to recall—remember the myths that are attached to those, okay? Maybe we'll go back to those . . . in a short while"). To accomplish these multiple tasks, Johnson must sometimes direct ("would someone do me a favor, please"), sometimes inform ("Christ was depicted as holding the lamb"), sometimes question ("The animals, which ones?"), and sometimes respond ("Holding the lamb?"; "Okay, that's good"). In at least one of her turns, we see three purposes working together:

> *Response:* "Okay, I couldn't remember that. The masks. The picture you're referring to really, aren't you?"
> *Inform:* "Christ was depicted as holding the lamb, the eyes if I'm remembering correctly from the very beginning of the book."
> *Question:* "Okay, anything else?"

During such discussions, then, the teachers were called upon to serve several purposes with their language, while students were usually asked only to inform.

But in other discussions, more often those in middle- or lower-track classrooms, the teachers used their turns largely to inform. We can see an example of these patterns in an excerpt from Carrie Anderson's middle-track discussion of John Hersey's *Hiroshima*.

> *Anderson:* Now did you get any names for Father Kinesorge's people?
> *Student:* Cieslik.
> *Student:* Cieslik.
> *Anderson:* Okay, let's get through those. Spell it to me.
> *Student:* C-i-e-s-l-i-k.
> *Anderson:* All right, Cieslik. I think Cieslik is going to come out bad. He's going to end up with all kinds of glass in his back. Do you know anything about getting a piece of glass in your skin?
> *Student:* It stays in and you can't get it out.
> *Anderson:* And it doesn't come out, right? It doesn't work out like a sliver will work back out. But glass doesn't. Glass keeps cutting and going and this guy's got a whole back full and listen, this is fantastic. I'm glad you're here right after lunch. They try to take him out of the city, see. He's got this back full of glass. It's still in there. They put him on this cart, belly down, with the glass and then they try to take him along a street that was like out in the front of school.
> *Student:* Blacktop.
> *Anderson:* Blacktop. Asphalt. And the asphalt heated up from that bomb drop and it's soupy and the road where it isn't blacktop is, it erupted and so they're going soup, soup, soup, soup, soup, and they go over a bump and they tip him off and that poor sucker. He lands on his—
> *Student:* Back.
> *Anderson:* Back, and it drives [the glass] even farther in. Poor Cieslik. Oh, I shouldn't get off on that. Okay, any other guys?

In most ways, this excerpt exemplifies the patterns in both teachers' and students' turns. Each of the students' turns here is short and each is clearly informative in purpose. More interesting, perhaps, is that each is intelligible only because of the context that Anderson's turns have built for it. "Cieslik" makes sense only if it is understood as an answer to Anderson's previous question. The same is true of "blacktop" and "back." In fact, the students' responses can be seen as slotting neatly into a framework that Anderson is building each time she holds the floor. Anderson builds that framework by acknowledging or repeating a student's contribution ("All right, Cieslik."), moving on to a longer stretch of exposition ("I think Cieslik is going to come out bad. He's going to end up with all kinds of glass in his back."), and then closing with a question ("Do you know anything about getting a piece of glass in your skin?").

But the nature of that framework, and not just its shape, seems most critical here. Anderson employs a kind of black humor in the excerpt "this is fantastic.

I'm glad you're here right after lunch" as a way of hooking her students into the text and making them visualize the admittedly awful details. Because of the way Anderson retells the episode and dramatizes Cieslik's suffering ("soup, soup, soup, . . . and they go over a bump and they tip him off and that poor sucker."), John Hersey in a way becomes Stephen King. But Anderson risks that for the opportunity of making vivid to her students the kinds of details that they might otherwise miss. She sacrifices, we might say, a certain measure of literary decorum in exchange for a measure of color and drama, and she does so by using her turns to provide a good deal of information to her students. We will look more closely now at the nature of that information.

Informative Statements

As we explain in Chapter 2, to examine the kinds of information that students and teachers exchanged in classroom discussions, each informative remark was first coded for the focus of information: "Classroom logistics," "Reading or quoting from text," or "Instructional focus." Those statements that were coded as instructional were further analyzed for knowledge sources drawn upon and the kind of reasoning employed.

The percentages of informative statements with an instructional focus are presented in Table 6. In general, teachers made instructional remarks 53.6 percent of the time, using the remainder of their statements to comment on classroom logistics or to read aloud from a text. About 90 percent of students' statements, meanwhile, had an instructional focus.

More interesting are the kinds of knowledge that teachers and students drew upon when making informative statements about the issues under discussion. The relevant data are summarized in Table 7. On the average, teachers and students drew most frequently on knowledge about the text during discussions: teachers focused on the text 64.8 percent of the time, and students 67.8 percent of the time. Neither teachers nor students focused often on personal or autobiographical knowledge (5.6 percent for teachers and 9.1 percent for students).

Teachers were more likely than their students to make statements about the biography of an author or the genre in which the author was working (5.6 percent for teachers and 2.1 percent for students). Teachers and students were about equally likely to make statements that drew on more general sources of knowledge, while teachers were slightly more likely than students to refer to previous instruction.

Because participants' statements most frequently focused on the text during discussions, we can additionally ask what kinds of reasoning they employed in making their informative remarks. The data for teachers and

Table 6

Percentage of Instructional Focus in Statements and Questions:
Percentage of Units by Speaker

	n of Units	Statements	n of Units	Questions
Upper track				
Teacher	2,338	58.9	1,087	83.1
Student	1,741	93.5	231	73.2
Middle track				
Teacher	5,172	37.3	1,549	75.2
Student	2,495	86.4	523	45.0
Lower track				
Teacher	3,439	74.7	1,209	76.3
Student	1,226	92.5	188	61.7
Average				
Teacher	10,949	53.6 (18.7)	3,845	77.8 (4.2)
Student	5,462	90.1 (3.8)	942	55.2 (14.2)

Note: Numbers in parentheses are standard deviations.

students are summarized in Table 8. In general, teachers were more likely to summarize or describe information than were their students (65.9 percent for teachers and 42.7 percent for students), while students were more likely to interpret information than were their teachers (41.1 percent for students and 26.6 percent for teachers). Neither group was likely to evaluate or to generalize.

Taken together, the analyses of knowledge source and kinds of reasoning in participants' informative statements provide another angle of vision on the teachers' and students' contributions to discussions. Teachers most often offered descriptive statements when they spoke, drawing on the text or more general sources of knowledge, perhaps to set the stage or to provide the context for the interpretive work of the discussion. Students, on the other hand, most often offered those interpretations when they held the floor. Though they also made descriptive statements, usually about the text, the most striking finding here is the relative proportion of descriptive and interpretive statements made by teachers and students during discussion.

We will see some of the reasons for these patterns in the analyses of the questions that teachers and students asked in the course of discussions.

Table 7

Knowledge Source for Informative Statements:
Percentage of Units by Speaker

	n of Units	Personal	Text	Context	General	Prior Instruction	Other
Upper track							
Teacher	2,338	5.8	50.4	7.4	21.5	6.2	8.5
Student	1,741	8.2	66.0	1.6	12.8	2.8	8.5
Middle track							
Teacher	1,942	8.8	61.3	7.0	4.8	6.9	11.2
Student	2,157	13.6	64.8	2.9	4.5	2.3	11.4
Lower track							
Teacher	2,570	3.0	78.4	3.3	5.9	6.2	2.3
Student	1,133	1.9	80.9	1.1	9.3	2.3	4.5
Average							
Teacher	6,850	5.6	64.8	5.6	10.3	6.4	6.8
Student	5,031	9.1	67.8	2.1	8.2	2.5	8.9

Questions

As with informative statements, questions asked by participants during discussions were first coded for focus: classroom logistics or instruction. Those questions coded as instructional were further analyzed for sources of knowledge and kinds of reasoning elicited. As Table 6 suggests, 77.8 percent of the teachers' questions had an instructional focus, while only 55.2 percent of the students' questions were addressed to the instructional material at hand; the remainder had to do with issues of homework, due dates, or other logistical concerns.

As Table 9 suggests, teachers and students were most likely to ask instructional questions that elicited knowledge about the text under study (76.5 percent for teachers and 69.9 percent for students). Participants were far less likely to ask questions that drew upon personal, contextual, or general knowledge.

As indicated in Table 10, the kinds of reasoning elicited by participants' questions were largely summary and interpretation; 45.9 percent of the teachers' questions and 54 percent of the students' questions were coded as summary, while 47.5 percent of the teachers' questions and 36.3 percent of the students' questions were coded as interpretive. Taken together, these two categories represented more than 80 percent of the questions asked by both

Table 8

Kinds of Reasoning for Informative Statements:
Percentage of Units by Speaker

	n of Units	Summary	Interpretation	Evaluation	General-ization	Other
Upper track						
Teacher	2,338	64.0	27.9	5.0	0.1	2.5
Student	1,741	39.6	43.5	9.2	1.0	6.6
Middle track						
Teacher	1,942	68.4	19.6	0.9	1.3	9.9
Student	2,157	54.3	28.9	0.1	2.7	13.6
Lower track						
Teacher	2,570	65.5	31.0	0.2	1.6	2.3
Student	1,133	24.8	61.4	0.3	9.1	4.4
Average						
Teacher	6,850	65.9	26.6	1.9	1.0	4.6
Student	5,031	42.7	41.1	2.9	3.7	9.3

teachers and students, and the general pattern held across each of the class-rooms studied.

General Patterns of Statements and Questions

With these trends before us, we can now examine more specifically the kinds of contributions made by the teachers and students during the classroom discussions. We can contrast, for example, the patterns in sources of knowledge and kinds of reasoning for both statements made and questions asked by participants in the course of those discussions. These contrasts are summarized in Table 11.

Perhaps the most obvious finding here is that the pattern of students' informative remarks reflects quite closely the pattern of teachers' questions. Teachers' questions were largely focused on the text (76.5 percent), and student's statements were generally focused on the text (67.8 percent). Nearly 46 percent of teachers' questions asked for description or summary, and 42.7 percent of the students' remarks were descriptive in nature. Almost 48 percent of teachers' questions asked for interpretation, and 41.1 percent of the students' remarks were interpretive. While these general averages again mask individual variation, and while such data do not indicate that the teachers' questions completely controlled the nature of student answers, the trend, at least, seems clear: students' informative remarks in these discussions were

Table 9

Knowledge Source for Questions:
Percentage of Units by Speaker

	n of Units	Personal	Text	Context	General	Other
Upper track						
Teacher	903	4.8	72.9	2.8	12.1	5.9
Student	166	2.4	56.0	1.2	17.5	22.9
Middle track						
Teacher	1,164	7.6	76.0	1.1	6.2	7.7
Student	235	9.4	72.8	0.8	5.5	1.5
Lower track						
Teacher	921	2.5	80.1	0.9	8.5	7.3
Student	116	0.9	81.0	4.3	10.3	3.5
Average						
Teacher	2,988	5.2	76.5	1.5	8.5	7.1
Student	517	5.4	69.9	1.7	10.0	12.9

reflective of, and often shaped by, the questions asked by teachers. Whatever else teachers' questions may have done, they seem to have established a framework that encouraged particular forms of language and particular ways of considering the texts under discussion.

A second general pattern here provides further suggestions as to how those frameworks were constructed. Teachers were more likely to describe than to interpret in making statements (65.9 percent versus 26.6 percent), but they were equally likely to ask descriptive and interpretive questions (about 46 percent for both). The basic pattern seems to be one of teachers using their statements to provide a descriptive background, drawing most often on textual knowledge, and then asking questions that elicited either more information or an interpretation of some aspect of the text under study.

We can see more clearly how teachers made descriptive statements to provide a background in this excerpt from Francis Connelly's upper-track class discussion of John Steinbeck's *The Grapes of Wrath*. Participants here are discussing the character of Jim Casey:

> *Connelly:* Who's the first one who sees [Casey]? Through whose eyes do we meet him?
>
> *Student:* [inaudible] Tom Joad.
>
> *Connelly:* Through Tom Joad, the main character. So through Tom we meet the preacher. And they talk. What do you know about the preacher? Maybe I shouldn't call him that. Why not? Why shouldn't I call him the preacher?

Table 10

Kinds of Reasoning for Questions:
Percentage of Units by Speaker

	n of Units	Summary	Interpretation	Evaluation	General-ization	Other
Upper track						
Teacher	903	37.4	53.5	7.6	0.1	0.1
Student	166	50.1	39.8	4.8	3.0	1.2
Middle track						
Teacher	1,164	65.2	30.4	0	1.5	2.9
Student	235	69.9	19.5	0	0	11.6
Lower track						
Teacher	921	28.4	64.3	0	4.2	3.0
Student	116	26.1	66.4	0	5.1	2.6
Average						
Teacher	2,988	45.9	47.5	2.0	2.0	2.2
Student	517	54.0	36.3	1.4	2.1	6.5

Student: He has strange ideas.

Connelly: He has strange ideas, a little strange.

Even though Connelly asks two questions in this exchange, we can already see how he uses his turns to flesh out the students' responses, providing more descriptive detail than the students offer. Tom Joad, for example, becomes "Tom Joad, the main character." A little later, Connelly continues to ask questions about Casey:

Connelly: He says I'm not a preacher anymore. Don't regard me as one. Why not?

Student: [inaudible]

Connelly: He what?

Student: Because he's been with women and—

Connelly: Because he sleeps with women, he thinks he's, he thinks he's a hypocrite to say he's a minister or preacher. Okay, that's a bit of it. What else? He doesn't want people to regard him as a minister. How do you find that out about him?

Student: He said it.

Connelly: He said it. "I don't wanna be a preacher. Not a preacher anymore." Tom said, "I remember you. You're the preacher man. You used to visit town when I was a boy, giv'n those hell-fire sermons in the tent. Got everybody jumpin' up and down. Said Alleluia! I been saved!

Table 11

Knowledge Source and Kinds of Reasoning for Statements and Questions:
Percentage of Units by Speaker

	Statements		Questions	
	Teacher	Student	Teacher	Student
Knowledge source				
Personal	5.6	9.1	5.2	5.4
Text	64.8	67.8	76.5	69.9
Context	5.6	2.1	1.5	1.7
General	10.3	8.2	8.5	10.0
Reasoning				
Summary	65.9	42.7	45.9	54.0
Interpretation	26.6	41.1	47.5	36.3
Evaluation	1.9	2.9	2.0	1.4
Generalization	1.0	3.7	2.0	2.1

or I'm a sinner. Come up front and be baptized with your sins." In the front of the—Where did he baptize them?

Student: In the church.

Connelly: Not in the church. In the ditch by the side of the road. Where there's some water, you know, caught from the rain. It's not exactly an area of lakes and rivers where he is. He baptized them in a ditch by the side of the road. Yes? And he had a good crowd of them. But he stopped doing that now, he explains to Tom, because there was some hypocrisy in it, he felt. There was something that wasn't right. And yet he still, he talked a lot, didn't he? He talks a great deal. He's the first one to say that. "Oh, yeah, I talk a lot. I'm not a preacher anymore, but I still talk a lot." Now what else does he do around the store besides talking? We meet him several times sitting behind the house while there was a meeting. What was he doing? All by his lonesome, he thinks. He's thinking. "I was thinking, I was puzzling it out. I was thinkin' about it." Time and again that refrain comes back to us. Um, what's his name, that preacher?

Though Connelly asks few questions here, the general pattern of his turns seems clear. He is, in a sense, retelling part of the story—the part relevant to the character the class is discussing. The students' statements, while few, are woven into that context, becoming a part of the summary that Connelly himself is providing.

We can see these patterns again by examining an excerpt from one of Jean Taggert's lower-track discussions of Arthur Miller's *Death of a Salesman*. Taggert has just asked about Willy Loman's dream:

Student: He has a dream for Biff to be great.

Teacher: To be great. To be a big star. To do something wonderful. What was Willy's dream for himself?

Student: Don't he want to get a raise from work or something, pay the bills?

Teacher: That's what he wants now at sixty. He's driving off the road. He's in terrible trouble. But at sixty, these were his problems. What were his dreams? What was his goal?

Student: To go with his brother?

Student: To make it big. To make it out of the jungle. That's what it says.

Teacher: That's what Ben did. Ben made it out of the jungle. And, you know, you just picked up on a metaphor: the jungle of life. Not that you have to literally go to the jungle, but all of life is a kind of jungle that you have to fight your way out of in order to succeed or make it big. Now he wants, Willy wants, to make it big. What else did he want? You can tell by his behavior. What was so important to him for his boys?

Student: To be better than everyone else.

Teacher: Yeah. What's the word that's used over and over again?

Student: Popular.

Teacher: To be popular. To be well liked. Popular.

Student: Now is that for him or for his kids?

Teacher: Well, I think he wanted it for himself, to be a salesman. Don't you? Or do you think it's just for Biff?

Student: No, I think—

Student: Well, if they knew his kids, they would know him too.

Teacher: That's one of the issues we have with our children. Sometimes the pressure we put on them to make it big is so that we get—

Student: But I thought he was—

Student: But he wasn't when he dies. Nobody was there. Nobody remembers him.

Teacher: This was his dream. It's called the American Dream. Now this is in the 30s that we're talking about. Do you think the American Dream to make it big, which I think is equivalent with rich, to be well liked, to be popular—What is also part of that? Be noticed for what you do in life? Is that still a dream that we have as people?

Taggert asks questions and makes statements in about equal measure here, but it is the nature of those statements and those questions that seems most distinctive. In general, the statements she makes are descriptive of the text or of the world outside of the text. Thus she says about Willy that at sixty "he's driving off the road. He's in terrible trouble"; about Willy's brother that "Ben made it out of the jungle"; about Biff that Willy "wants him to make it big." She points out a metaphor ("the jungle of life") and defines one version of the American Dream ("which I think is equivalent with rich, to be well liked, to be popular"). She uses her turns in part to set the stage for the largely

Table 12

Response: Percentage of Units for Teachers

	Acknow-ledge	Restate	Evaluation Positive	Evaluation Negative	Ask for Expla-nation	Elabo-ration	Other
Upper track ($n = 882$)	13.6	35.1	4.5	0.1	10.1	19.2	0.1
Middle track ($n = 891$)	24.7	38.1	16.2	3.7	9.9	7.4	0
Lower track ($n = 596$)	7.2	45.5	21.4	2.4	12.4	10.1	0
Average ($N = 2,369$)	16.2	38.8	13.2	2.0	12.8	12.5	0

interpretive questions that she asks: "What was his goal?" "What was so important to him for his boys?" "Do you think it's just for Biff?" The students' statements, meanwhile, are woven into the context Taggert provides. They are largely answers to her questions ("To go with his brother"; "To be better than everyone else"). Only once does a student ask a question ("Now is that for him or for his kids?"), and Taggert quickly answers it ("Well, I think he wanted it for himself") before turning it back to the student ("Or do you think it's just for Biff?").

Teachers did more in their turns, however, than provide information and ask questions. At least part of the time they were responding to the contributions of their students; that is, they acknowledged, restated, evaluated, or otherwise reacted to the nature, quality, or substance of students' remarks. We will turn now to the analysis of those responses.

Responses

Students' responses were so few in number (less than 5 percent of their total remarks) that they were not analyzed further. Teachers' responses were coded within seven categories. The relevant data are summarized in Table 12.

Perhaps the most surprising trend here is how relatively seldom teachers' responses directly evaluated the quality of their students' contributions. Earlier studies of classroom discourse (e.g., Cazden, 1988; Mehan, 1979; studies conducted largely in elementary classrooms) had found such evaluative responses pervasive—part of a three-turn sequence of teacher question–student answer–teacher evaluation. In the discussions examined here, however, although there was some variation, teachers on average offered evaluations only about 15 percent of the time when they were responding to their students.

More typical of teachers' responses in these discussions was an effort to restate what students had said. Such statements comprised 38.8 percent of the total responses. Other kinds of response occurred with generally equal frequency: acknowledgment, 16.2 percent; evaluation, 15.2 percent; requests for explanation or clarification, 12.8 percent; and efforts to elaborate upon students' contributions, 12.5 percent.

Taken as a whole, this pattern of teacher response helps complete the portrait of teachers' and students' contributions that has thus far emerged. The teachers' responses pulled students' remarks into the ongoing discourse. By acknowledging them, repeating them, or elaborating upon them, teachers wove the varying statements and questions offered by students into a coherent oral "text" whose organization might quickly break down were it not for the explicit, transitional purpose served by the responses.

We can see this transitional purpose more clearly in several responses offered by teachers in the discussions. The first is from Grace Whitman's upper-track class discussion of Dickens's *Great Expectations:*

> *Student:* It's hard to read for Pip, because most of the time Pip is talking in the narrative. Like if you go through the narrative that what he's saying and you've got to pick a couple of words that he's saying.
>
> *Whitman:* I gave you a hard task, didn't I? A kind of dramatic scene where they didn't show Pip's words in exact quotations. He uses what we call an indirect statement. "I said that," and you have to do the transposing. And I realize that's a real challenge. We'll see how you got that worked today.

Here Whitman uses a student's particular problem as an opportunity to teach something about narrative. She introduces the notion of indirect statements in narrative at the same time she validates the difficulty of the student's task. We can see another variation on the pattern in the following excerpt from Laura Peters's lower-track discussion of *Of Mice and Men.* The class is working on a description of the scenery Steinbeck includes at the beginning of the book:

> *Teacher:* How does he describe the foothills? What adjectives does he use?
>
> *Student:* Golden?
>
> *Teacher:* He talks about the golden foothills. Now, tell me, what does that mean? How can foothills be golden?
>
> *Student:* The sun is setting and the light is reflecting off the trees.
>
> *Teacher:* The sun was setting and the light is reflecting off the trees. We know that the sun is setting because on the next page we're told it's getting toward evening. And the sun's kind of shining off in the distance making those foothills look golden. Now how about the valley side. The

side with the trees. What does he say about the trees? What type of trees are they and how do they look?

Student: They're willows and they're fresh with green and spring.

Teacher: Okay, he talks about the valley side being lined with willows. With willow trees. And he says they're fresh and green with every spring. And then he says something about the sycamore trees which are also on this one side of the water. Where the trees are. You probably didn't understand this line. But can anybody tell me what the line is?

Student: "With mottled white . . ."

Teacher: The line is actually "the sycamores with mottled, white, recumbent limbs." And branches. Okay. The question is what does that mean? It happens to be a very specific line about what the trees are like but if you don't have a couple of vocabulary words you might have trouble. "The sycamore trees with mottled limbs." Does anyone know what the word "mottled" means?

Student: Spotted, colored, more than one color.

Teacher: Exactly. More than one color. And then they are "recumbent." Anybody know "recumbent"?

Student: Reclining?

Teacher: Exactly. I saw an ad over the weekend for a recumbent exercise bike. And I think you can sort of sit back and lie back and pedal. I don't know if it's more relaxing or you work harder. I don't know what the details are. But the word "recumbent" means "reclining, resting."

In each of her turns here, Peters repeats or elaborates upon a student's contribution as a transition to another question ("He talks about the golden foothills. Now tell me, what does that mean?") or to another piece of information ("The sun was setting. . . . We know that the sun is setting because on the next page we're told it's getting toward evening. And the sun's kind of shining off in the distance"). The teacher's responses serve to acknowledge a student's remark while at the same time using it as a point of departure for further exposition. Though students' individual contributions are sometimes brief, consisting only of one or more words ("golden"; "spotted, colored, more than one color"), they are contextualized by the questions that come before and the responses that come after, and are thereby woven into a discourse that the teacher is actively shaping.

General Discussion

The analyses reported in this chapter have examined the patterns of discourse during classroom discussion, and more especially have explored the kinds of knowledge that participants used and produced in the course of discussions. Several general patterns emerged from the study.

1. In terms of the sheer quantity of talk, teachers dominated most of the large-group discussions we observed. On the average, the floor was returned to the teacher after each student's contribution, and, again on the average, teachers' turns were two to five times longer than students' turns.

2. Teachers used their turns for a number of purposes. At times they directed or explicitly orchestrated classroom activities, but most of the time they informed, questioned, and responded to students' contributions. Students, on the other hand, usually made about one remark per turn, and that remark was almost always informative in purpose.

3. Students' informative remarks were largely reflective of the kinds of questions teachers asked, and both questions and statements were dominated by the description and interpretation of textual information.

4. Teachers used their responses to students' contributions to weave the discussion as a whole into a coherent and sustained examination of two or three general topics. Students' contributions were not generally evaluated individually as answers to specific questions, as in a recitation. Rather, those contributions were most often repeated, questioned, or elaborated upon in ways that pulled them into the ongoing discussion. The discussions stayed "on track" largely because teachers used their responses to students' remarks as occasions for making transitions from one turn to another, from one question to another. The teacher ultimately controlled the direction, the pace, and the organization in most of the discussions we observed.

In a very important sense, these patterns are not surprising. On the one hand, virtually every previous study of classroom discourse (e.g., Barnes, 1969; Bellack et al., 1966; Cazden, 1988; Mehan, 1979) has documented the controlling features of teacher talk and the sheer quantity of that talk during most classroom discussions. If anything, the results from this study suggest a shift away from the "persistence of the recitation" (Hoetker & Ahlbrand, 1969) as a central pattern of classroom discourse, for here teachers balanced purely factual questions with interpretive questions and seldom simply evaluated their students' answers.

On the other hand, we should not be surprised by the centrality of questions and remarks that focused on the text under study and that emphasized the description and interpretation of that text. Applebee (1993) and Purves (1981) have documented the persistence of an "academic" approach to literature in American high schools, and both the longstanding influence of the New Criticism (e.g., Kirkpatrick, 1972) and the longstanding strategy of "close reading" as an instructional tool (Culler, 1980) suggest that we would probably find comparable patterns in many literature classrooms. Indeed, given the intelligence with which the teachers in this study articulated their goals for discussion, it is likely that the classes we observed were representative of some of the best instruction in literature to be found.

But those classes were representative of a certain kind of instruction, and the patterns that we found there are surprising, and to that extent troubling, largely in light of the goals and purposes that the teachers themselves expressed. We seldom, for example, found evidence that discussions were moving toward a point where teachers could remove themselves, disappear, and "watch it happen." We seldom saw evidence that students were moving much beyond answering their teachers' questions (however carefully those questions may have been framed) or that they were engaging with the literature on a personal level. Their responses tended to be relatively brief and unelaborated, their questions relatively few. Both individually and as a group, they frequently cooperated with the teacher in organizing and sustaining an examination of the text, but the direction and context of that examination were usually in the teacher's control. The students' role was to help develop an interpretation, rarely to construct or defend an interpretation of their own. While the goal expressed by teachers was to help students toward a point where they could individually develop a response to the text, we saw in the classrooms we observed few occasions where students could practice such interpretive skills, at least during large-group discussions.

Conclusion

What seems most central in these studies of classroom discussions is not the differences across ability levels, but their fundamental similarity. At least two explanations could account for the consistency of these patterns. On the one hand, the similarities suggest that the conventions governing classroom discussions are powerful and that they may often operate in spite of the student audience or the teacher's stated intentions. Presented with the complicated task of managing the talk among a large group of participants and shaping that talk into coherence, teachers may feel that they have no choice but to take the role we have seen them take here. Research on teaching has generated few alternative models for how large-group discussions might proceed, and the chances are great that the teachers themselves have seldom experienced those alternatives in their own schooling. Working from experience and logistical necessity, then, teachers leading any group of students in a discussion might find themselves responding, informing, and questioning—controlling the talk, even when that talk is meant to engage students in more personal forms of exploration.

Such an argument might explain the general similarities of discussions across contexts, but it does not account finally for the very specific and very profound constraints that teachers working in lower-track classrooms were facing when they discussed literature in school. The teachers we studied did not simply lack alternative strategies. That problem was compounded by the fact that the students themselves were so alienated from school, from the texts they were asked to read there, and from the kinds of talk that took place there that the teachers had to provide a supportive structure for them before the process of personal engagement could even begin. Consider for instance the following exchange between Veronica Carter and one of her students during a discussion of "Raymond's Run." Carter had just asked the class if they had found any problems in the story:

> *Student:* What do you mean by problems?
>
> *Teacher:* Oh, problems. See, I guess what I'm thinking of is I found some problems in the story—something that I didn't like that Squeaky said or the way Squeaky thought about something or something that doesn't make sense with you. Is there any problem with the way she tells the story? That's what I mean. That's what I'm trying to have you think about.
>
> *Student:* And write that down on paper?
>
> *Teacher:* You got it. How did this story make you feel? What were you feeling when you heard this story?
>
> *Student:* It didn't make me feel like nothing.

We might point out here that Carter's role is central. We might suggest that she is responding, informing, and questioning as other teachers typically do. We might argue that the student's contributions are minimal. But what seems most telling about the exchange, brief as it is, is the lengths to which Carter goes in inviting her students to speak their minds. We might describe the exchange, in fact, as a teacher-centered dialogue in the service of a student-centered response. Carter is not interested in telling her students the specific problems that she has seen in the story. She is not concerned that they take away the "central" problems or the "most important" problems. She wants only for them to engage with the text in a way that matters to them. But even at that level she is met with "It didn't make me feel like nothing." And so she must begin again, attempting to arouse her students' interest. To get them beyond that "nothing," she must lead, provoke, dramatize, providing the "security information" that these students may need to develop a personal response. She ends by employing many of the strategies others employ, but her intentions are different, her audience is different, and the difficulties she faces will not be solved by simple answers. Indeed, as our next study suggests, using small-group discussions in the study of literature, one answer often offered to teachers as a way to increase student involvement, is not so simple as it may first appear.

4 Small-Group Discussions: Alternatives to and Extensions of Teacher-Led Discussions

The research reported in Chapter 3 reveals the tensions experienced by teachers as they discuss literature with their students. In our own teaching at both the high school and university levels, we have often found ourselves in similar situations, compelled on the one hand to cover a certain amount of material and teach particular methods of understanding texts and concerned on the other hand with letting students play a leading role in determining the content and process of discussions. We have learned, like the teachers in Chapter 3, that simple solutions to these tensions are not available. Like the teachers described so far, we have sought to make ourselves "invisible" in the classroom, withdrawing our influence and direction in discussions as students demonstrate more independence in their transactions with texts; and like those teachers, we have met with resistance to our efforts, at times from students unaccustomed to the role we ask them to play, at times from our own desire to meet our instructional goals.

In spite of the tensions and resistance, we have maintained our belief in the importance of student engagement in both the content and process of discussion. Like many teachers, we have searched for ways to increase that engagement. One way we have tried to foster student authority in our classrooms has been to provide students with opportunities to discuss literature in small groups where they are presumably free of our influence. Our reasoning and our experiences have told us that the small-group setting can empower students in their explorations of literature and help move them towards independence in their ability to have meaningful transactions with texts.

Our view of the benefits of small groups has been supported by much anecdotal evidence shared in the faculty lounge and found in publications such as the *English Journal.* Many researchers, too, have documented the benefits of small groups, although for the most part research has looked at the products of group work rather than the processes engaged in by students. The study of small-group products, while informative to some degree, has its limitations; for in the end, as DiPardo and Freedman (1987) point out, "We know little about precisely why groups work when they do, or perhaps more importantly, what accounts for their failures" (p. 2). While many teachers and researchers (including ourselves) have often regarded small-group work as somewhat of a panacea for promoting student authority, we also know from our own experiences that small groups "just don't seem to work" on many occasions. Slavin (1989) states the problem succinctly: "It is not enough simply to tell students to work together" (p. 233).

Most research on small groups (e.g., Slavin, 1989) has focused on how to set up and administer them, with attention to delegating responsibility, providing incentives, and other managerial considerations. Yet we have found that in some situations even the most careful planning of structure and rewards does not prevent small groups from going awry. In investigating small groups, then, we sought to look for other factors that might influence the ways in which they work (see Smagorinsky & Fly, 1993).

Our understanding of social theories of learning helped provide the framework for our study. Rather than looking at managerial considerations (for example, the delegation of responsibilities) that presumably could apply to any small-group situation, we decided to look at *situational factors* that might affect the processes of small groups. The work of Vygotsky (1978, 1986) is central to our focus on the instructional context of small-group work. Vygotsky stresses the social and cultural aspects of learning, in particular the ways in which a learner internalizes the reality offered by the external world. We have already discussed these processes in our review of Bakhtin's notion of speech genres. But even in a given speech genre there is room for variation. Our study of small-group discussions of literature considers both the ways in which a variety of teachers enact the speech genre of literary discussions and the ways in which students are affected by these individual enactments.

The study was designed so that each of four teachers would use small groups at the same juncture in an instructional sequence, would use the same literature, would use similar management procedures, and would focus the group task on the same problem. More specifically, the research was motivated by these questions: Might individual classrooms develop particular patterns of discourse that influence the specific ways in which students learn to think and talk about literature? Are there variations on the speech genre of literary discussions that could help account for the ways in which students in different classrooms learn to think and talk about literature? What pedagogical moves do teachers make that enable students to adopt particular ways of thinking and speaking about literature?

Method

The Setting

The study took place in a large midwestern suburban high school with a four-year enrollment of 2,681. The community includes a range of racial groups, with the student body representing white (69.2 percent), African

American (23.1 percent), Asian-Pacific Islander (4.7 percent), Hispanic (2.8 percent), and Native American (0.2 percent) citizens. Within these racial groups there is also considerable diversity in terms of ethnicity and income.

The School

The community has traditionally placed a high value on education, investing $8,053 per pupil in 1989–90. More than 85 percent of the graduates of the class of 1989 enrolled in some sort of college or trade-technical school. In 1988–89 students from the school scored well above national averages on the ACT and SAT, with a mean ACT score of 21.1 (2.5 points over the national average) and a mean combined score on the SAT of 989 (86 points over the national average).

Eighty-five percent of the faculty have earned a master's degree, with 73 percent having earned thirty additional hours. The typical faculty member has taught for seventeen years, fourteen in the district. The teachers in the present study represent the norms regarding educational level, but as a group are slightly less experienced than the district's average teacher.

The school follows the practice of ability grouping or tracking. The mainstream students are placed in one of three tracks, known as honors, regular, or basic, with an advanced placement program available for seniors. The regular track reflects quite closely the racial makeup of the overall student body. The basic track is disproportionately populated by minority students, the honors track by white. The 1989–90 sophomore honors courses, for instance, which are included in this study, had a black enrollment of 5.1 percent.

Participants in the Study

Participants in the study came from four sophomore classes in the school. Three of the classes were regular track, one honors. The classes were selected by soliciting volunteers from among the seven teachers—one of them the researcher—who taught regular-track sophomores. Three of the seven agreed to participate, and at the last minute one of these teachers withdrew from the study. At that point the researcher, who had originally piloted the data collection procedures with his own students, decided to become a teacher-researcher and include the data from his own classes in the study to replace those of the teacher who had withdrawn. The fourth teacher also taught sophomores, but in the honors track. The study had originally intended to focus on regular-track students, but when one honors teacher expressed an interest in participating in the research, his classes were taped and included in the analysis.

Had this been a strictly experimental study, the inclusion of the researcher's classes would be problematic. However, the research was designed as exploratory, looking for relationships rather than identifying "best" methods, and so the classes of the researcher simply added one more set of transcripts to the analysis. Furthermore, the inclusion of the researcher's own discussions provided a unique professional opportunity to reflect on his own teaching in a highly systematic way, resulting in a greater understanding of the processes involved in his teaching. In retrospect, the researcher's decision to pilot the materials with his own class and the one teacher's sudden withdrawal from the project proved to be serendipitous, allowing for great personal reflection and understanding on his part.

The teachers in the study (identified through pseudonyms) included one woman and three men and represented distinct instructional styles. Among their distinguishing characteristics were the following:

1. *Mr. Harris* taught a regular-track section. He used small groups for prewriting activities about once every two weeks. He organized his small groups heterogeneously (that is, by sorting them according to his perception of their ability so that the groups were in his judgment evenly matched).

2. *Mr. Stone* taught a regular-track section. He used small groups for various purposes several times each week. He organized his small groups by student choice (that is, by letting students constitute their own groups).

3. *Ms. Sanders* taught a regular-track section. She rarely if ever used small groups in her class. She organized her small groups randomly (that is, by arbitrarily appointing members to groups).

4. *Mr. Azarov* taught the honors section. He used small groups in his classes at least once each week for both writing and discussing literature. He organized his small groups heterogeneously.

Instructional Context

The study examines small groups as they are employed at a particular point in an instructional sequence: following a teacher-led introduction to the reading of thematically related short stories. The theory motivating the placement of small groups at this juncture is Bruner's (1975) notion of *instructional scaffolding*, derived from Vygotsky's (1978, 1986) theories concerning learning in social environments. Bruner's metaphor of an instructional scaffold refers to the initial support a teacher (in or out of school) provides for learners in acquiring a skill or concept, with the support gradually withdrawn as the learner internalizes the knowledge and learns to perform independently. Some theorists (DiPardo & Freedman, 1988; Dyson, 1990) have criticized the metaphor of a scaffold as being unduly rigid, suggesting a top-down flow of knowledge. The image of an unyielding scaffold, they say, does not take into account the transactional nature of social learning central to Vygotsky's perspective and underestimates the activity of the learner in internalizing concepts. Although we are more content with the metaphor of the scaffold than these critics are, our research—if we may look ahead to our conclusions—supports their view that the relationship between teachers and learners must involve activity and flexibility on everyone's part.

For this study, each teacher led a discussion on a short story concerning a coming-of-age experience in the first class session, and the students followed the teacher-led discussion with a small-group discussion of a thematically related story. Our analysis of small groups does *not* attempt to find anything characteristic of small groups as an independent, decontextualized learning event. Rather, our purpose is to examine them *in situ;* that is, as students engage in small groups as part of their participation in greater classroom discourse. The sequence that we examine—teachers supporting student interpretations in a whole-class discussion, followed by small-group discussions of a thematically related story—represents a potential instructional scaffold or, if the metaphor offends, represents a potential transactional relationship intended to support students' learning in the early stages of concept formation.

The study did not attempt to measure the effects of the small-group discussions on "literary understanding," which is an increasingly disputed concept in the world of theory, if not practice. Rather, the study focused on the relationships between the patterns of discourse in the teacher-led and small-group discussions. The small-group discussions, therefore, were analyzed according to the ways in which students appeared to adopt the ways of thinking and talking about the literature that their teachers provided for them, at least as indicated in the limited sample of classes and discussions analyzed in this research.

Methods and Materials

The discussions came in the normal course of instruction during a thematic unit on coming-of-age stories. The sophomore curriculum was organized around thematic units of instruction, with the stories coming from a course anthology. A pilot study had identified two stories from the anthology, "Peter Two" by Irwin Shaw and "The Bridge" by Nicolai Chukovski, as roughly comparable in difficulty, as measured by student responses to a series of questions based on the taxonomy developed by Hillocks and Ludlow (1984).

Each class session was tape-recorded. For the small-group sessions, each class was divided into five groups of four or five students, with each small group recorded separately. Thus each teacher contributed taped sessions of one teacher-led discussion and five small-group discussions.

From the total set of data, transcripts for this study were selected as follows:

1. *Teacher-led discussions:* To identify the patterns of discourse of each classroom when the teacher presided over discussions, we analyzed the teacher-led class discussion that initiated the instructional sequence. The teacher-led discussions, we assumed, would give us a sample of the type of talk that students had become accustomed to hearing and participating in over the first two months of school and would provide us with specific examples of how teachers led their students in discussions of coming-of-age stories.

2. *Small-group discussions:* The data provided five small-group discussions from each class; we selected two from each teacher for analysis by using a table of random numbers. Of the randomly selected discussions, some tapes were difficult to transcribe because of excessive background noise, and others were unusable because of tape-recorder malfunctions. Inaudible tapes were replaced with other tapes selected randomly from the same class.

Procedures

Each class began with attendance and a brief content quiz to ensure that students had read the story, leaving about thirty to thirty-five minutes for teacher-led discussions and twenty to thirty minutes for small-group discussions. The small-group sessions tended to be shorter because the teacher needed to provide instructions on how to arrange the groups, how to operate the recorders, and what students should do in their groups.

Students in all classes were in a modified version of the "Completely Cooperative" groups described by Stodolsky (1984): they shared a common goal (interpreting the story), participated in common means and activities (responding to a story heuristic), and were expected to contribute about equally. The modification involved having each student turn in an individual response to the questions on the heuristic rather than having a joint product evaluated. This modification was introduced to promote participation in the discussions.

The story heuristic used by students in the small groups was derived from the sophomore curriculum. As noted, this curriculum was organized around thematic literature units, each developed around a set of key questions that could be applied across the literature in the unit. The heuristic asked the key questions that had been developed for the coming-of-age unit:

1. What values and characteristics does the protagonist have at the beginning of the story that you would call "immature"? Give examples and explain why they are immature.

2. What key incident causes the character to change? Why does this incident cause change? In other words, what makes this incident so much more powerful than other experiences the protagonist has had, so powerful that it causes a major change?

3. How does the protagonist change from the beginning of the story to the end? Why does the protagonist change? Give examples to support your answer.

4. Is the protagonist better off or worse off because of these changes? Why?

The heuristic—representing the emphasis of the curriculum—required students to engage in analytical and argumentative responses that typify much classroom discussion of literature, with an emphasis on making generalizations about the text supported by proof and examining structural aspects of the story to identify changes in the central characters.

For the teacher-led discussions, the teachers were asked to use this same heuristic as a basis for whatever discussion they might ordinarily conduct. The study therefore captured teachers as they adapted the framework of the curriculum to their own approaches to teaching. Teachers were advised that the study hoped to capture discussion under "normal" conditions in which their personalities, styles, and methods showed through. They were thus encouraged to cover the same issues as the small groups while remaining faithful to the curriculum, retaining their instructional style and interests, and fitting the stories in with their own interpretive emphases.

Analysis

Tapes of the discussions were transcribed by a professional typist. A research assistant then played the tapes back and checked them against the transcripts, revising them accordingly. The coding system used to analyze the tapes is described in Chapter 2.

For the present study we modified the basic coding system by developing an additional category for both "Knowledge Source" and "Kind of Reasoning." Teachers in this study made certain discussion procedures explicit, thus necessitating a "Procedural" knowledge category. For instance, at one point in his discussion Mr. Azarov said, "There is something else that we need to ask." Here he is drawing attention to the process of discussion itself, explicitly telling students that in order to gain the greatest insight possible they need to pose additional questions. Such statements could then receive a coding of "Metastatement" as a kind of reasoning, in that they were stepping outside the discussion to make a statement about the process of discussion.

Following extensive piloting of the coding system on a separate set of transcripts, we used a sample of four of the twelve transcripts for a reliability check, with independent raters agreeing on 92 percent of the coding decisions, and final coding decisions determined through a discussion of those units coded differently.

Results

The coding of the transcripts suggests that the kinds of talk engaged in by teachers in whole-class discussions does influence the ways in which students talk about literature in small groups. The four teachers in this study were all quite different from each other. Students of teachers who were highly interactive in whole-class discussions tended to adopt certain patterns of speech and thought in their small-group discussions. However, when a teacher modeled interpretive methods in whole-class discussions without engaging students in the process of interpretation, students neither adopted the teacher's patterns of speech or thought nor engaged in any other extended means of discussing the literature when working in small groups.

The sections that follow present the characteristics of both the teacher-led and small-group discussions of all four teachers, identifying relationships between the patterns of discourse in the two settings as revealed by the application of the coding system.

MR. HARRIS

Teacher-Led Discussion

Mr. Harris led his discussion in what has been called a "frontal" (Goodlad, 1984) or "presentational" (Hillocks, 1986) manner; that is, his remarks governed the discussion both in terms of their length and frequency and in terms of the way in which his perspective shaped the direction of the discussion. Mr. Harris's discussion was characterized by several traits: (1) he provided for his students an appropriate extratextual interpretive framework by (a) sharing lengthy anecdotes from his personal experiences and (b) generating relevant examples from the students' presumed world of experience; and (2) he directed the students to a particular way of reading the story. The following sections illustrate each of these traits with excerpts from the transcripts.

Providing an Extratextual Interpretive Framework

Drawing on Personal Knowledge. Mr. Harris had the style of a raconteur, spinning long stories about his own past that were related to the experiences of the literary characters. He appeared to be modeling for his students how to generate a personal response to literature through the consideration of a related story. The following excerpt is typical of the many expansive personal anecdotes he shared in order to connect his own past with the dilemmas of the characters. When coded, many of the following units were identified as having a personal knowledge source as he provided for the student his frame of reference in reading the story:

> *Mr. Harris:* Jim, what was your feeling about the protagonist? Was he unrealistically portrayed in the beginning? Did you think his reaction to the bad things that were happening to him was pretty strange?
>
> *Jim:* No, I thought they were probably just about as close to real life as possible and in particular where his parents were feeling insecure because they are not sure who to trust or who they can depend on.
>
> *Mr. Harris:* Like the roles had been changed.
>
> *Jim:* Yeah, turn your whole life upside down.
>
> *Mr. Harris:* I always feel superior to someone who's undergone a bad situation and think, well, I would react one way and then I think I don't know how I would react. I can remember thinking specifically about a teacher here at [the high school] who had cancer and I thought he was reacting pretty bizarrely through the whole situation and doing some kind of strange things. One night, right after the middle part of Christmas, this was right before Christmas break, I was bowling with him, and a friend of mine had a sudden emergency surgery. He went to bed feeling fine and in the middle of the night had an attack and had to go to the hospital and had an emergency operation. By noon the next day, he was out of the operation and doing pretty well. I was telling him about this because he knew this other person too, and I thought he might be interested. And I said, boy isn't it weird to go to bed and twelve hours later all of this has happened to you and you are having this serious operation but you have gone through okay and there you are back in your hospital room and you think twelve hours ago I was okay. And he said, and he was very cold when he said this, he said if I could start walking right now to Joliet to a hospital that would give me one chance out of a hundred to recover that I would either die on the operating table or recover and be okay, I would start walking out that door right now. And maybe I would freeze to death on my way, and maybe I would make it, but I would take that chance out of a hundred chances. And three weeks later he was dead. And I thought, boy, here I was feeling so superior judging his reactions and his sort of bizarre reactions to things and I didn't even slightly understand what he was going through. Frieda?
>
> *Frieda:* How did he die?
>
> *Mr. Harris:* He just got weaker and weaker and died. He was a shop teacher, and he had cancer.
>
> *Pam:* Of what?
>
> *Mr. Harris:* Cancer. Just pervaded everything.

Mr. Harris continued on in this fashion for quite some time, occupying nineteen out of the next twenty communication units with further descriptions of his experiences, with the only student contribution being a question asking him for details about his story. Following the conclusion of his personal digression, the discussion returned to the literature.

This excerpt from the transcript illustrates one of the predominant features of Mr. Harris's discussion-leading style: the tendency to share long, detailed experiences from his past that were related to the experiences of the literary characters. The frequency with which Mr. Harris provided extratextual information to his students is reported in Table 13. The data reveal that he *informed* students about extratextual knowledge more than 30 times as often as he *questioned* them and provided more than 20 times as many informational statements as did his students. Through the predominance of such codes, it appears as though Mr. Harris was attempting to model for his students a means of making personal connections between their own experiences and those of the literary characters, much in the manner that Rosenblatt (1978) has argued is central to an aesthetic response to literature.

Drawing on Relevant General Knowledge. Mr. Harris's tendency to provide an appropriate extratextual framework was also illustrated by the broad social or conceptual context he developed to help students interpret the story. By providing these external contexts he seemed intent on illustrating for students how the story represented experiences common to them all and how it might therefore help them better understand their own lives. In the following excerpt, for instance, Mr. Harris took an incident from the story and provided a relevant correlative example from the students' own worlds. Many of the following statements were coded as appealing to general knowledge as a source of information (that is, one available from popular culture or the media). The codes reveal once again that Mr. Harris sought to go outside the story to provide a context for interpretation.

> *Mr. Harris:* Roxanne, what happens after he jumps into the water?
> *Roxanne:* He saves the girl.
> *Mr. Harris:* Is it an easy saving?
> *Roxanne:* No, because the current pulls them under.
> *Mr. Harris:* That is described in great detail. Why do you suppose the author describes the saving in such great detail? Heather.
> *Heather:* I wasn't here that day. I didn't read the story.
> *Mr. Harris:* I did announce it after you came in, but I didn't [inaudible]
> *Karla:* [inaudible]
> *Mr. Harris:* It has to be arduous for anything to be important. It has to be difficult. For example, if it were easy to play the guitar, we would all be Eric Clapton. But all of us probably have sat down with either our guitar

Table 13

Inform-Question Codes Coupled with Extratextual Codes

	Harris	Sanders	Stone	Azarov
Teacher-led discussion				
Total extratextual codes: teacher	97	88	54	10
Total extratextual codes: students	4	30	31	2
Teacher: inform	94	62	34	7
Teacher: question	3	26	20	3
Student: inform	4	30	31	2
Ratio				
Teacher: inform/ teacher: question	31.33:1	2.38:1	1.7:1	2.33:1
Ratio				
Teacher inform/ student: inform	23.5:1	2.07:1	1.1:1	3.5:1
Small-group discussion				
Mean extratextual codes: inform	2.5	18.0	22	8.5
Mean extratextual codes: question	0.5	5.5	14	3.0
Mean extratextual codes: total	3.0	23.5	36	11.5

or somebody else's guitar. The first thing you find out is that it sort of hurts and it is hard to keep the frets down. So you get one chord and you struggle for a while, like, row, row your boat. You got to change it, and it is difficult. Now, if it is a matter of just hopping off a two-foot bridge into three feet of water and saying, don't be silly, you're all right honey, that is not going to be something that changes him very much.

In modeling how to generate both a personal and a conceptual framework to aid students' interpretation of the story, Mr. Harris provided them with the sort of context many educators believe readers should establish to inform their response to literature: he was connecting the problems of the character to both his own experiences and those of relevant figures from the students' culture. He then made an explicit link between the extratextual references and the experiences of the literary characters. Yet the data also reveal that the students played a primarily passive role in generating the interpretive framework; their statements were brief, and the only questions they posed were requests for Mr.

Harris to tell more about his experiences. Their role as observers did not involve them in the act of generating a framework for understanding the decisions of the literary characters. Like the students described in Chapter 3, they did not join the teacher in helping to set the terms for the general direction of the discussion. As the data from their small-group discussions suggest, this passive role did not appear to provide them with procedures for connecting the story to their own network of personal and general knowledge; or at least they did not see how to apply that knowledge within the framework provided by the story heuristic.

Setting the Direction of the Discussion

In addition to providing a social and experiential context for the problems in the literature, Mr. Harris also assumed the role of asking students questions about the story itself. The transcript includes no occasions when the students addressed one another or spoke consecutively; the transcript reveals a steady pattern of teacher-student-teacher-student turns. Aside from asking Mr. Harris questions about his own experiences, the students posed no other questions during the discussion. Like the students described in Chapter 3, their primary role was to give brief answers to Mr. Harris's questions, following which he would either pose another question, elaborate on their answers, or talk at length about issues he felt were important in understanding the text. The frequency and length of teacher and student turns are listed in Table 14. Mr. Harris's turns were more than three times as long as those of his students. The following excerpt typifies the manner in which he took over interpretive responsibilities, in terms of both the length of his turns and the direction he provided for the interpretation of the story:

> *Mr. Harris:* But in the act of the saving itself, one particular thing happens between the two people. Can you remember what it is? Erin.
>
> *Erin:* It sounds like she starts to like him even though she doesn't know him.
>
> *Mr. Harris:* She likes him, and she likes him because—
>
> *Debbie:* He saved her.
>
> *Mr. Harris:* Even before he has saved her?
>
> *Erin:* He chased her.
>
> *Mr. Harris:* He chased her. She falls in the water. She struggles and now they are really in trouble. They both almost drown. She stops struggling, why? Lee.
>
> *Lee:* She trusts him.
>
> *Mr. Harris:* What does she say, and how do you know she trusts him?
>
> *Lee:* Because she says, I'll do anything you say.
>
> *Mr. Harris:* Yeah. She says I will do anything you say. How many times do you think anyone has said something that they really mean that goes

Table 14

Units, Turns, and Episodes

	Harris	Sanders	Stone	Azarov
Whole-class discussion				
Teacher turns	61	116	101	98
Student turns	61	128	112	113
Teacher units	235	371	238	244
Student units	75	171	147	174
Teacher				
Units per turn	3.85	3.20	2.36	2.49
Student				
Units per turn	1.23	1.33	1.31	1.54
Ratio				
Teacher units per turn/				
student units per turn	3.13:1	2.4:1	1.8:1	1.61:1
Total no. episodes	1	4	2	3
Mean turns per episode	122.0	61.0	106.5	73.3
Mean units per episode	310.0	135.2	192.5	139.2
Small-group discussion				
Mean turns per discussion	88.5	155.0	287.0	186.5
Mean units per discussion	131.0	212.5	402.5	244.5
Mean no. episodes	4.5	5.0	3.5	3.5
Mean turns per episode	19.64	31.0	82.0	53.28
Mean units per episode	29.11	42.5	115.0	69.85

as far as saying I trust you, I will do anything you say? That confers—go ahead, Erin.

Erin: No one has ever said it.

Mr. Harris: No one has ever said it. That confers a kind of immediate responsibility. Well, he has two things he could do. He could try to save her. He also might drown, that possibility is great. Or, he could just let her go and let her drown. No one will ever know. He goes up and gets his bicycle which isn't even wet, pedals back home. Before they find her body, he is on his way to Russia, to Moscow. Probably no one is ever going to connect him with anything like that. The girl will be found a couple of days later. Her bicycle will be found. They will assume that she was driving across and fell off. He gets away scot-free. But he doesn't do it.

In leading his discussions, Mr. Harris assumed the major responsibility for providing context, posing questions, and elaborating and synthesizing student responses. Presumably, his modeling of these important analytic procedures would teach his students a means of facilitating their own exploration of the literary characters' dilemma. As the analysis of his small-group discussions will show, however, the critics of the scaffolding metaphor make an important point in stressing the "dynamically interpersonal, flexible" character of learning (DiPardo & Freedman, 1988, p. 130). The teaching of Mr. Harris seems to illustrate a rigid scaffold that provides support without encouraging student involvement. Dyson (1990) has argued that the scaffolding metaphor suggests a "vertical" relationship between teacher and students (p. 204) and "directs our attention to the teacher's official intentions" (p. 210). Her alternative metaphor of "weaving" is more "horizontal" (p. 204), placing greater emphasis on the learner's activity in an instructional transaction. Mr. Harris's relationship with his students appeared to be vertical in that he initiated and directed the substance of the discussion. Next we will examine the extent to which his focal role enabled his students to adopt appropriate interpretive procedures when exploring literature on their own.

Small-Group Discussions

Regardless of the metaphor we adopt, we must assume that the goal of the teacher's instructional method is to empower students to engage in subsequent independent activity that is fulfilling and enriching. In order for Mr. Harris's discussion to have enhanced the students' experiences with subsequently read literature, they would need to have adopted some sorts of procedures for connecting relevant personal experiences to the characters, for seeking a broader social context through which to view the story, and for prompting elaboration of their views.

Of the students in the study, however, Mr. Harris's students generated the fewest personal experiences, provided the most minimal social context, and engaged in the least elaboration of their responses. They would address themselves immediately to the questions on the story heuristic, generate an acceptable answer, and move on to the next question regardless of the sufficiency of the response. Their discussions were governed by a pragmatic need to complete the assignment and were marked by little effort to explore the issues in depth or frame their interpretation in terms of either their own personal experiences or a larger social or conceptual context. Students' turns were perfunctory and directed towards the production of a brief response to the question.

The following episode is typical of the extent of discussion among Mr. Harris's small groups and includes the entirety of their exploration of the causes of the character's change:

Gail: "What key incident causes the character to change?"

Barbie: When they—

Ellen: When he sees the man pointing the gun.

Gail: Somebody else say something.

Ellen: I don't know.

Gail: Does anyone else think anything else? Why do you think he changed? Judy, why do you think he changed? [Background, overheard from another group's discussion: You want to eat grapes. Then he ate the seeds of the peaches. That is sick.]

Barbie: He ate the seeds of peaches?

Ellen: No, grapes.

Barbie: But [the person in the other group] said that.

Judy: No just grapes. Okay. I guess it's the incident like when he thought he was a hero and then the next-door neighbor, he heard the screaming of the next-door neighbor. And then—go to the part when he hears the screaming of the next-door neighbor.

Barbie: Yeah.

Judy: And then after that, cause he thought he was a big hero, and then he didn't do anything to save her—

Barbie: He realized he wasn't a hero.

Judy: Right.

Barbie: I don't understand why they were like so happy together the next day.

Judy: I know, that's what I don't understand. Maybe he imagined it.

Barbie: That could be it, Judy.

Judy: Huh?

Barbie: That could be it. It could be a total dream.

Judy: Good.

This episode suggests that Mr. Harris's students developed few procedures for engaging in the type of thinking required by the heuristic. Rather, they settled on the first plausible answer and then moved on to the next question. Data on the students' small-group discussions are included in Tables 13 and 14. Table 13 reveals that, in their small-group discussions, Mr. Harris's students averaged only three extratextual remarks, well below the totals found in the other teachers' classes. Table 14 reveals that both the turns and units in Mr. Harris's small groups were substantially fewer than those of the students of the other teachers.

The coding of the transcripts suggests that Mr. Harris's style did not help his students discuss literature in the sort of analytic-argumentative fashion required by the heuristic. Two explanations are possible. One is that his storytelling style did not engage students sufficiently in the process of response, thus causing their attention to drift. Csikszentmihalyi and Larson (1984) found that passive activities such as listening to the teacher or other students talk resulted in low degrees of affect, mental activation, cognitive efficiency, and motivation, with students in teacher-led discussions and lectures devoting only 40 percent of their thoughts to what others were saying (see also Bloom, 1954). In a follow-up study, Csikszentmihalyi, Rathunde, and Wahlaen (1993) studied an honors history class in which the teacher was lecturing about Genghis Khan's invasion of China. Of the twenty-seven students in the class, only two were thinking about China; and of those two, one was thinking about Chinese food and the other was wondering why Chinese men wore their hair in ponytails. Possibly, Mr. Harris's students had difficulty adopting his procedures because they were not sufficiently engaged in the process to keep them attentive.

The other explanation is that Mr. Harris's storytelling style did not prepare students for conducting the more formal analysis of an independent story required by the heuristic. Although he did typically return to analysis in his discussions, the analysis usually came in response to the stories he would tell. As we will report in Chapter 5, adult participants in reading clubs frequently engaged in autobiographical digressions and spoke of them quite fondly. One wonders how their small-group discussions might have gone had the task been to generate a personal story parallel to that of the protagonist, rather than to analyze the story with conventional generalizations and support.

Mr. Harris appears to have had laudable intentions in demonstrating to his students how he thinks in his transactions with literature. In many ways, his response to the literature is much more in line with Rosenblatt's theories than with those of the New Critics; he informs his view of the characters with reflections about deeply personal incidents from his past that relate to the experiences of the literary figures. If we accept the need for student engagement as part of their learning of the process of reflection, however, he does not appear to be teaching them how to engage in such consideration themselves, at least as they demonstrate in their small-group discussions. The discussions from Mr. Harris's classes, therefore, suggest that theorists need to consider more than just the worthiness of the approach to finding meaning in literature a teacher brings to the classroom (that is, transactional, New Critical, Marxist, and other perspectives). The process of discussion is critical to students' learning. If students are not sufficiently active in participating in the discussions, they may not learn to apply a literary theory once they are free of the teacher's direct guidance.

MR. STONE

Teacher-Led Discussion

Mr. Stone's discussions were quite different from those of Mr. Harris. Mr. Stone's discussions were characterized by several traits: (1) he prompted students to generate an extratextual framework to inform an interpretation of the story (rather than modeling his own thinking processes); (2) he prompted students to elaborate their contributions to the discussion; and (3) he made the process of literary analysis explicit by stepping outside the discussion and talking about procedures for interpreting literature. The following sections illustrate each of these traits with excerpts from the transcripts.

Prompting Students to Generate an Extratextual Interpretive Framework

Mr. Stone attempted to frame the interpretation of the story in a particular conceptual context: a definition of maturity through which to judge the character's change during the story. Unlike Mr. Harris, who attempted to create this broader context by modeling it for students through reflection on his own experiences, Mr. Stone established this conceptual framework through references to previous class discussions about maturity and through questions that prodded students to draw on their own general knowledge about relevant behavior. The excerpt that follows illustrates the conceptual context that he created at the outset of the discussion through references to previous class discussions, to students' general knowledge, and to generalizations about mature behavior. These influences focused students' attention on the importance of viewing the story in terms of a broad extratextual framework.

> *Mr. Stone:* Let's start to think about this story in terms of the structure that we are working with, that being we are using a definition to analyze the change in the character from the beginning of the story to the end and we are looking at a significant event in the story that is responsible for this change. Who can start us off with if, who could start us off by telling us something about the character at the beginning of the story, particularly in terms of some definition of the concept of maturity? Come on now. You all just wrote me an event that starts off the story, you all just did that in your quizzes presumably, so all of you must have something in mind. Thank you, Patsy.
>
> *Patsy:* He thought it was mature to, well, he was eating grapes and staying up late with, he was eating grapes and grape seeds and staying up late and watching TV without his mother's approval.
>
> *Mr. Stone:* Okay, eating grapes and seeds and a couple of other examples. He was staying up late.
>
> *Patsy:* Yeah.
>
> *Mr. Stone:* And he was also—

Patsy: Watching TV.

Mr. Stone: And watching TV when told not to. And all these fall into the category of what?

Patsy: Huh?

Mr. Stone: These all have in common something.

Patsy: Well, disobeying.

Mr. Stone: Okay, he was disobeying his mother. All right. Now what can you do with this? In other words, what are you trying to tell us by bringing up these points?

Patsy: That he thought he was mature by disobeying his mother. He thought it made him a more mature person and older by doing things he wasn't supposed to do.

Mr. Stone: Thought he was mature through these acts. Okay, and what does Patsy think? Do you agree with it?

Patsy: What? No.

Mr. Stone: Why not?

Patsy: He was just showing how immature he is by doing that.

Mr. Stone: And what criterion of a definition of maturity are you using to make this judgment? Why is this, you are saying that this is, in fact, immature even though he thought he was mature? That is what you are saying, right?

Patsy: Yes.

Mr. Stone: Why? You are saying he is immature because of something and that because is your definition. And what is it about your definition that allows you to make this judgment?

Patsy: Well, he—

Mr. Stone: Can Gary help you out?

Patsy: Yes.

Gary: He's disrespecting the law.

Mr. Stone: Disrespecting the law. Is that a—

Gary: It is kind of like what his mother's saying is the law.

Mr. Stone: Patsy has already said that.

Gary: It is like breaking the law.

Mr. Stone: And that is a sign of immaturity. A sign of maturity is to obey the law is what you say. So obey the law says Gary's definition, and response to that?

This excerpt is typical of the teacher's attempts to get students to frame their interpretation of the story in terms of their understanding of the concept of maturity. His discussion-leading agenda is quite similar to Mr. Harris's, who also strove to expand the context of the story to include both a personal and a social framework. The difference between the patterns in the two discussions is one more of process than of focus. Mr. Harris sought to provide the broader framework of the story for the students through extensive reflection on his own knowledge and experiences. Mr. Stone, on the other hand, attempted to get students to generate their own context, as suggested by the greater frequency of "Question" codes in the first category of codes for general or personal knowledge statements (see Table 13). Mr. Stone, therefore, appears to be modeling for the students *a means of prompting* the generation of a broader social and conceptual context, rather than modeling the production of the context itself.

Prompting Students to Elaborate Their Contributions

Mr. Stone prompted students to elaborate not only a broader interpretive context but their other contributions to the discussion as well. One recurring pattern in his transcript was the presence of "Respond-Request Elaboration" codes in which he requested that the student pursue the interpretation further, as illustrated in the following excerpt:

> *Mr. Stone:* What was different about this incident, what was unique about this incident? This experience, was it a real life-threatening incident as opposed to, as Maggie said, his previous television? He lived kind of a cartoon life up to that point. And now he changes. He is now mature as evidenced by what, as measured by which criteria? Heather.
>
> *Heather:* The next day after they wouldn't let Mrs. Chalmers in, and he left with Mrs. Chalmers and he turned on all of the lights in the house, in the apartment. The next day, he got up and saw that everything was okay, but there was another thing. When he came back, he turned on the TV and saw the spy show was on, and so he decided not to watch anymore.
>
> *Mr. Stone:* And he?
>
> *Heather:* And he turned the TV off.
>
> *Mr. Stone:* And he turned the TV off. Is that all, Heather? Or do you have more?
>
> *Lucy:* He also faced reality.
>
> *Mr. Stone:* He faced reality, how? I want to see your evidence of his facing reality.
>
> *Female student:* By saying this is just for kids.
>
> *Mr. Stone:* By saying this is just for kids. Lucy is saying that that is an act of facing reality. How?
>
> *Lucy:* Because he is starting to realize that stuff is pretty much fake. It's not really what happened. Well, sometimes it might, but—
>
> *Mr. Stone:* So by recognizing the fantasy nature of TV, separating the fantasy nature of TV from the reality of the hallway, you are saying that he is then facing reality?
>
> *Lucy:* Yes.

The frequency with which Mr. Stone requested elaborations from his students is presented in Table 15. More than 8 percent of his remarks were prompts for students to develop their ideas further, as illustrated in the pre-

Table 15

Respond-Request Elaboration Codes: Whole-Class Discussions

	Harris	Sanders	Stone	Azarov
Respond-request elaboration codes	4	16	20	37
% of respond-request elaboration codes among all codes	1.7	4.3	8.4	15.2

vious excerpt. Taken in the context of his attempt to get students to generate an extratextual interpretive framework, his method of requesting elaboration appears to be part of a general concern for getting students to formulate a response to the literature in their own terms and for engaging them in analytic processes rather than modeling a means of interpretation.

Making Analytic Procedures Explicit

Another recurring pattern in Mr. Stone's transcript was his tendency to refer to the process of discussion itself. In the transcripts, these units were coded as having a procedural knowledge source. Through these statements, Mr. Stone appeared to be making analytic procedures explicit to students, as in the following excerpt:

> *Mr. Stone:* Okay, now what does that tell you about him? For some reason we are bringing these up and saying they are evidence that he is mature, isn't that what you are saying? That he is mature. We are saying that all of these things help us to classify this behavior as immature behavior, but I don't see any reason to make that classification based on the definition that we have up there so far. What do we need to do? Does anyone disagree with the judgment that all of this is immature? Is there anyone contesting that? What's missing now? Something is missing. We don't have anything to make the judgment by so we need to decide what part of the definition allows us to make that judgment. Is your hand up, Gary?
>
> *Gary:* You could say for a definition that bragging about stuff is being immature, or boasting about it would be a sign of immaturity.
>
> *Mr. Stone:* Bragging or boasting says Gary. Well, note that that would be a definition of immature. What does a mature person do?
>
> *Gary:* They don't need to brag.
>
> *Mr. Stone:* A sign of maturity is not bragging.
>
> *Gary:* They already know who they are.
>
> *Mr. Stone:* Oh, now you just said something different. Because they what?
>
> *Gary:* They already know who they are.

Table 16

Procedural Codes

	Harris	Sanders	Stone	Azarov
Whole-class discussions				
Procedural codes	0	5	25	9
Small-group discussions				
Mean procedural codes	0	1	14	2

> *Mr. Stone:* So it sounds as though you are saying the criterion should be self-knowledge. The reason for that, Gary, as you pointed out so astutely, is that the mature person has self-knowledge. Any response to that?

In posing such questions as "What do we need to do?" and "What's missing now?," Mr. Stone pointed out to students that, in order to pursue their consideration of the story, they needed to make a procedural move: "We need to decide what part of the definition allows us to make that judgment." He appeared to be attempting to provide students with interpretive strategies—such as using definitions of concepts in order to evaluate characters—that they might apply in their independent analyses. The frequency with which all four teachers made analytic procedures explicit is detailed in Table 16. Both Mr. Stone and his students discussed the process of analysis far more frequently than did the other teachers and students in the study.

Overall, Mr. Stone appeared to be attempting to engage his students in the process of analysis by encouraging them to provide the framework for literary analysis, elaborate their responses, and develop knowledge of a process of literary analysis. He seemed intent on involving students in analytic discourse. As the analysis of his small-group discussions will illustrate, his interactive approach appeared to be effective in helping students develop a language for interpretation when left on their own in small groups.

Small-Group Discussions

Mr. Stone's small groups generated episodes that were long and included extended probing of the issues under discussion. The patterns of discourse in his small groups paralleled those of the whole-class discussion Mr. Stone led. The small-group discussions of his students suggest that they did adopt some of the procedures he had made explicit in his discussion. The following excerpt, for instance, illustrates students' generation of a broader conceptual context for interpreting the story. The four students also appear to have developed the procedure of requesting elaborations or defenses of one another's interpretations, as suggested by the "Why?" and "Why not?" statements that were coded "Respond-Request Elaboration":

> *Rose:* Okay, the protagonist Costia had, there was no self-confidence.
>
> *Heather:* What did you put?
>
> *Rose:* I put the protagonist Costia had no self-confidence. Um, shy—It says something else about him too. He liked to be alone, and he didn't want to talk to anyone. Kind of like being an outcast.
>
> *Alicia:* Being antisocial.
>
> *Rose:* No. So, antisocial. He didn't like to express himself to anybody. How do you say that? And he didn't feel comfortable. I guess that's kind of antisocial.
>
> *Patsy:* Uh, how do you—is antisocial hyphenated?
>
> *Alicia:* Yeah. Is he actually immature for these, I mean, how can you be immature?
>
> *Patsy:* It's, it's kind of like when you're not really mature until you're—
>
> *Alicia:* Until you're social?
>
> *Rose:* Well, yes.
>
> *Alicia:* So, a person's shy so they're—social?
>
> *Patsy:* It takes maturity to be social.
>
> *Alicia:* No.
>
> *Patsy:* Yes it does.
>
> *Alicia:* No.
>
> *Patsy:* Well, a four-year-old is not mature and does she come, or he or she come out and like say, "Hi, my name is so-and-so. Would you come out and play with me?"
>
> *Rose:* Yeah.
>
> *Alicia:* Yeah, but I mean, no, I don't think you have to be social to be mature. I think there are lots of people who are. But you're not as successful if you keep to yourself.
>
> *Patsy:* Yeah. But that—
>
> *Rose:* But you are not as successful when you are, when you keep to yourself.
>
> *Alicia:* So you have to be successful to be mature, too?
>
> Rose: Yes.
>
> *Alicia:* Why?
>
> *Rose:* I mean, not really successful, I mean, you have to—
>
> *Alicia:* In what way successful?
>
> *Rose:* I don't mean like aspiring, I mean like you don't have to be rich and a billionaire or anything.
>
> *Alicia:* Yes.
>
> *Rose:* You just have to like, you can work in a bookstore and be successful, I mean, it depends on what your standards are.

Alicia: Yeah. But if you worked in a bookstore and you were shy and you were antisocial, you're still not mature?

Rose: You really wouldn't be.

Alicia: Why? Yeah, but I don't understand why.

Rose: Working in a bookstore then.

Alicia: Why not?

Rose: I mean, because how—

Alicia: You can be antisocial and work in a bookstore.

Rose: How can you get all the way up to where you want to be? How can you like, get a store, how can you get everything if you're antisocial, you're shy?

Patsy: Yeah. If you keep to yourself and you don't want to learn anything.

Alicia: Yeah, I know. But to be antisocial, you don't have to be—to be antisocial, how social are we talking?

Patsy: A hermit, okay. A hermit, he's very antisocial.

Alicia: Yeah, I know. But you say he can be immature.

Patsy: He's very immature.

Rose: Oh, you're not mature until you can—

Alicia: Are we talking antisocial as not having any friends?

Rose: No.

Alicia: Or antisocial not being able to talk to anyone, because social—

Rose: Keeping, yeah, and not being—

Patsy: Keeping to yourself. Keeping to yourself.

Alicia: Are you sure it would be antisocial, though?

Rose: No. Go like this. The protagonist had no self-confidence. He was very shy and kept to himself most of the time.

The students in this small group engaged in a pattern quite similar to the one established in the teacher-led discussion, with students prompting one another to clarify their interpretation of the story in terms of a broader social and conceptual context (see Table 13). As revealed in Table 14, Mr. Stone's small groups, compared with those of the other teachers, engaged in the longest discussions, as measured by both turns taken and communication units identified. If we value the sort of transaction illustrated in this excerpt and documented in the tables, then we might conclude that the teacher's efforts to provide prompts to students and make them aware of the interpretive process helped to enable them to discuss the story in depth and interpret it in terms of their general and personal knowledge. We should note, too, that Mr. Stone's emphasis on examining change in the character was quite consistent with the focus of the story heuristic, which likely contributed to the students' transfer of the procedures from the large-group setting to the small-group discussion.

One conclusion we might draw from the relationship between his teacher-led and small-group discussions is that teachers need to be attentive to the scaffolding that students need for particular tasks if they want them to succeed at those tasks.

MS. SANDERS

Teacher-Led Discussion

Ms. Sanders exhibited some of the tensions that characterized the discussions reported in Chapter 3. On the one hand, she took a lower percentage of turns in leading her discussion than did Mr. Harris and initiated her discussion by asking students to identify confusing areas of the story in need of exploration. On the other hand, soon after soliciting student response to the story she controlled the direction of the discussion and made judgments on what constituted an acceptable interpretation. She seemed caught between conflicting purposes for her role in leading discussions. Ms. Sanders's discussions were characterized by several traits: (1) she initiated her discussion by soliciting students' affective responses to the story in order to identify points of confusion; (2) she prompted students to elaborate their contributions to the discussion; (3) she led students towards a predetermined interpretation of the story by (a) certifying responses of which she approved and (b) posing questions that directed students towards a particular reading of the story; and (4) she played the role of authority, providing an elaborated interpretation when students' answers were insufficient and when students indicated they were confused. The sections that follow illustrate each of these traits with excerpts from the transcripts.

Initiating Discussion by Soliciting Affective Responses

Ms. Sanders began her discussion by asking her students how they felt about the story:

> *Ms. Sanders:* So how many of you liked the story "Peter II"?
> *Brad:* That was dumb.
> *Ms. Sanders:* Oh, do you have to influence the whole class with your opinion? Now no one is going to raise their hand. No one liked it? No one's brave enough to say that they liked it?
> *Melissa:* I liked it a lot.
> *Ms. Sanders:* Did you really not like it at all?
> *Student:* I didn't like it.
> *Student:* I didn't like it at all.
> *Student:* It was okay.

Ms. Sanders: Can you tell me in some kind of intelligent way why you didn't like it, why you thought it was stupid? John.

John: I didn't understand it.

Ms. Sanders: The end, or the whole thing?

John: No, the part with the lady and the guy. Was it a dream? Because the next day, she wasn't beat up or anything.

Male student: Yeah, and she was fine. I mean back to normal.

Ms. Sanders: I would appreciate rather than just giving him an answer, getting some of your thoughts out fairly coherently. So you thought it was confusing. You thought it was unrealistic. Why?

Male student: Like you said, she had no marks on her [inaudible].

Ms. Sanders: Ned.

Ned: I just didn't like it. I couldn't understand like how the night before, he was going to shoot her, and then the next day they were fine.

Ms. Sanders: How many found that aspect of it to be highly unrealistic? Oh, wow. Is your hand up, or are you just waving your homework? So no big deal one way or another? You didn't like it particularly but you didn't really hate it. Did you find it confusing?

Female student: Yes.

Ms. Sanders: Yes, Denny.

Denny: I didn't know if it was imagination or not.

Ms. Sanders: That is a very common question, and I think, not a bad one, not at all. I think it happened, so before we get to those points that are really good ones, let's backtrack just a little bit. Why is he called Peter II? Let's just get a few of these literal comprehension things.

In searching for "literal comprehension things," Ms. Sanders asked how Peter II had gotten his nickname, and then she moved the discussion to Peter's reliance on television as a source of reality.

She had opened her discussion by seeking an affective response to the story that pointed to areas of confusion, with students then identifying parts of the story that they did not like because they did not understand them. A resolution of these perplexing junctures presumably would lead to a better appreciation of the story and a more positive response on the part of the students. She did not return to the junctures the student identified until much later in the discussion, however.

Ms. Sanders's approach appears to have helped her identify points in the story that had been confusing to students and appears to have yielded to students the initiative for locating the parts of the story most in need of discussion and resolution. Yet she quickly took back the initiative in determining when the class would discuss those points. She seems caught amidst many of the tensions reported by the teachers interviewed in Chapter 3: on the one hand she ceded authority to students in identifying problematic parts of the story to discuss, yet on the other hand she made her students' concerns secondary to her own beliefs about which parts of the story most merited their attention. The following sections give further evidence of the tensions that characterized her discussions.

Prompting Students to Elaborate Their Contributions

Ms. Sanders displayed a second trait indicating her attention to students' perspectives in discussing the story: she would prompt them to elaborate their contributions to the discussion. The frequency with which she encouraged students to develop their thoughts is presented in Table 15. She did so slightly less often than Mr. Stone, but considerably more often than Mr. Harris. The following excerpt illustrates the manner in which she prompted students to elaborate their ideas:

> *Ms. Sanders:* Danny, what do you think?
>
> *Danny:* I was just thinking how unrealistic it is.
>
> *Ms. Sanders:* What?
>
> *Danny:* How you can't really be in such a fight and have a gun the night before and the next morning be so in love.
>
> *Ms. Sanders:* Which is not reality?
>
> *Danny:* The morning. There is no way. I mean, you think that maybe he should have shot her or she left. And the reason that the boy didn't like understand this, is because it is he saw those shows, and on the shows, the end is always like someone is dead.
>
> *Ms. Sanders:* Or—
>
> *Danny:* Or hurt and leave him.
>
> *Ms. Sanders:* Or—
>
> *Danny:* Happy ending.

Her use of "Or—" served to prompt students to elaborate their thoughts, showing a concern for involving students in the development of the interpretation. As the next section shows, however, the authority granted to them had its boundaries. The students were encouraged to pursue an interpretation as long as it stayed within the limits of what Ms. Sanders believed to be an acceptable interpretation. Once again we see the "doubleness" that characterizes the teaching of literature, where teachers are caught between the needs to yield control to students but at the same time "get them somewhere" with their interpretations.

Leading Students to a Predetermined Interpretation

Ms. Sanders's discussions were characterized by a tension over the locus of control in discussions: to a degree she involved students in generating the substance of discussions, as just described; and at the same time she exerted control over the way in which that substance was discussed. The next sections examine the ways in which Ms. Sanders used her own reading of the story to shape students' interpretations.

Certifying Approved Responses. Ms. Sanders's responses to students' interpretations indicate that she preferred some answers to others. In the following excerpt, for instance, when students answered her questions with ideas that departed from her preferred interpretation, she accepted their responses as perhaps plausible, yet she did not endorse them:

> *Female student:* You say that Peter does not like—it could be the author was putting that of an experience he had to go through.
>
> *Ms. Sanders:* Possible. All right. Let me get back to something that I don't think was quite there. I think that Peter II could have handled and accepted and not been so disillusioned by the Chalmers's experience if what?
>
> *Female student:* If he had seen his parents fight.
>
> *Ms. Sanders:* That. If he had had the experience. Obviously, I was thinking he grew up in a home where there wasn't that kind of fighting, so it was shocking to him as opposed to no big deal. You know, parents fight all the time, and I am sure that that was a possibility, yeah.
>
> *Male student:* Maybe if he hadn't watched so much TV, all the shows.
>
> *Ms. Sanders:* That is possible too.

In this sequence she admitted the possibility that the students' responses might be right, but did not certify them with her approval; their responses were "possible," yet she continued to pose questions in search of another answer. In the following excerpt, however, her responses to student interpretations indicate that the students had hit upon an answer of which she approved. Rather than following up with additional questions to solicit a better answer, she tended to give her approval and then elaborate on the responses that fit in with her own reading of the story:

> *Ms. Sanders:* Why doesn't he like comedies? Did you understand that? It was very subtle, how they said it. Yes.
>
> *Male student:* I don't think he really understood the jokes.
>
> *Ms. Sanders:* Exactly right. He says, oh, they are always talking about income tax and stuff like that. They were talking about much more sophisticated things and he didn't understand the humor. He was how old?
>
> *Chorus:* Thirteen.
>
> *Ms. Sanders:* And he was in a thirteen-year-old—I mean, I am sure that comedians were not from "Saturday Night Live" or stuff like that. They would tell jokes about things that he just didn't understand and therefore found it boring. He liked the hero stuff, the superman stuff, the James Bond stuff, all those kinds of things that were exciting, and that had appeal. Of course, he had great desire to be like them. So then comes the Peter the Great incident with the cap. His confidence is boosted after that.

What does he start doing after that? Tom, do you remember? I know that's a real vague question.

Tom: He terms it as being fearless, by staying in the dark.

Ms. Sanders: Good. Why would that be fear? What does he do?

Tom: He would go in the kitchen, and purposely turns out the light and seems to be afraid of the dark. And he is just trying to overcome the fear.

Ms. Sanders: Good. What else does he do to try to bolster his self-image and stuff? Mark.

Mark: He does five push-ups every night.

Ms. Sanders: Right. He starts doing push-ups and is really into that.

In these excerpts, Ms. Sanders had a particular interpretation in mind when she responded to student contributions, one no doubt arrived at through prior readings and discussions of the story. Her *acknowledgment* of a remark signaled to the students that a response was perhaps plausible, but not sufficient in terms of the direction of the discussion, and suggested that they continue searching for better answers and interpretations. Her *positive* response to a student comment signaled that an answer was acceptable and the discussion could move forward. Ms. Sanders's own reading of the story determined the interpretation the class would pursue, and the nature of her response to student contributions informed them of when their interpretations were in line with hers and how the discussion could then proceed.

Directing Students to a Particular Reading. For the most part, Ms. Sanders's questions to students about the story elicited particular answers and elaborations. The sequence that follows is typical of the patterns of interaction she established in drawing out information about the story. The statements Ms. Sanders made that were coded "Inform" tended to elaborate on student responses, yet the *questions* that she posed tended not to arise from student insights but to direct them to additional issues in the text that she felt were important:

Ms. Sanders: Do you remember what the author says he noticed right before he did in fact open the door? It was a small detail.

Male student: He noticed he wasn't so fearless.

Ms. Sanders: Okay, that too but I am talking about something else. Alice.

Alice: His arms.

Ms. Sanders: What about them?

Alice: They're skinny.

Ms. Sanders: Right. He notices his reflection in the mirror and he notices how thin his arms are right before he is there, and this is doing five push-ups a day. So he notices a very different feeling between how he felt in a hypothetical situation, and how he feels in reality when he hears danger. However, he doesn't cower away. What does he do? He opens the door. And what happens, Andrea?

Andrea: He says [quotes from text]. Then he closed the door back.

Ms. Sanders: Well, what does he see? Why does he close the door?

Andrea: He sees Mr. Chalmers with a gun and Mrs. Chalmers was screaming.

Ms. Sanders: What was his experience with these people beforehand?

Andrea: He thought they were, the lady always waved, and—

Ms. Sanders: Do you remember what he says the man reminds him of? Small detail. Ron.

Ron: A principal.

Ms. Sanders: Reminds him of a principal. A real safe, probably authority, secure kind of person. And the woman always looked like she what?

Chorus: Came out of the beauty parlor.

In this excerpt Ms. Sanders took a strong role in directing students in the manner of their inquiry into the text and its meaning through her assumption of the role of question-poser and in her endorsements of responses of which she approved. Her questions determined the substance and structured the direction of the discussion and appeared to have clear answers. The questions she asked did not emerge from student contributions—did not build on the substance of student responses—but served to direct the class to points that she believed were important to cover.

Playing the Role of Authority

Toward the end of the discussion, the students revealed how dependent they were on Ms. Sanders as they began to ask her for her interpretation:

Ms. Sanders: He was put on the spot where he had to put up or shut up. Either he was going to be fearless and do something, or he was going to be a thirteen-year-old kid who would close the door. And what he did is what any thirteen-year-old would do. What are you going to do? When someone is in a fight, you are going to close the door. I'm not only— What about any age? You are going to close the door.

Male student: Why didn't he call the police?

Ms. Sanders: I don't know, I don't know.

Male student: Wasn't he like scared because he wasn't supposed to be up so late or something?

Ms. Sanders: Yeah, but sure, I don't know why. I don't know if it is an inconsistency in the story or if it is something that I am missing. It is certainly the most logical. It seems that any of us would have closed the door, gone to the phone and called the police.

In this excerpt the students, when unable to understand the story, asked the teacher to provide an interpretation. Ms. Sanders shared their perplexity concerning the reason behind the character's behavior and the question went unresolved. The students' dependence on Ms. Sanders to provide an authoritative reading of the story, however, was apparent in the way they turned to her to solve the problem, and in the way the students did not participate in the generation of a solution.

As Table 14 shows, Ms. Sanders occupied the middle ground relative to the other teachers in terms of the extent to which she controlled the floor in her discussions. In terms of frequency, she spoke more often than her students, but did not occupy the floor nearly as much as did Mr. Harris. In terms of the substance of the discussion, she exercised considerable authority in leading the students towards a particular interpretation of the story, yet allowed them to identify the parts of the story in need of discussion and admitted to them her own uncertainty in understanding certain ambiguous junctures. Her discussion is not so neatly amenable to a classification such as "presentational" in that she determined the direction of the discussion but encouraged the students to talk within the boundaries she had set. In their small-group discussions, her students had a difficult time leading themselves in the sort of analysis specified by the heuristic, yet engaged in extended discussion when abandoning the heuristic and responding affectively to the story. The following section details the processes of her students' small-group discussions.

Small-Group Discussions

Ms. Sanders's small groups began their discussions in a manner similar to those of Mr. Harris; that is, they provided brief, unelaborated responses to the questions until they had generated a satisfactory answer and then moved along to the next question without refining or reconsidering their responses. Like the students in Mr. Harris's groups, these students appeared to have taken a pragmatic approach to the assignment, producing what they felt was an acceptable answer and then moving along to the next question.

Ms. Sanders's groups differed from Mr. Harris's, however, in their discussions following their completion of what they perceived to be their assignment. At this point they would initiate a new discussion about the story, distinct from the one in response to the questions, in which they sought one another's affective responses to the stories. Typically their feelings about the story revealed points of confusion that they would then discuss and try to resolve. Their affective response, therefore, appeared to serve as a means through which they identified and discussed parts of the story they had not understood clearly. In this regard the students appeared to have adopted a pattern of thought from Ms. Sanders's discussion-leading approach, using affective response as a means of identifying problematic parts of the story in need of resolution.

The students of Ms. Sanders began their small-group work with brief responses to the questions on the story heuristic, seeming to seek a quick, acceptable answer to the questions. Here, for instance, is a typical episode in response to one of the questions:

> *Rex:* What values and characteristics does the protagonist have?
> *Tess:* Definitely immature.
> *Alice:* Yeah, he was hiding in the bushes.
> *Rex:* He was hiding in the bushes and still riding that bike. He rode that bike the whole time.
> *Tess:* So?
> *Jasper:* He was scared of her.
> *Rex:* Yeah, he was scared.
> *Alice:* And he didn't like want to leave and everything.
> *Tess:* He didn't want to grow up.
> *Rex:* Yeah.

The other episodes in which the students discussed the questions were similarly perfunctory (see Table 14). The next excerpt illustrates how the discussion changed, however, when they finished with the questions on the heuristic and began to generate their own questions about the text. One of the groups under study engaged in a lengthy discussion (45 turns) built around their affective responses to the story. The episode includes sequences such as the following:

> *Alice:* Well, why didn't you like it?
> *Tess:* It was hard to read. It was boring.
> *Rex:* It was.
> *Tess:* There was no point to it, really.
> *Alice:* Yes there was, how he changed his life.
> *Rex:* So we don't care about him changing his life.
> *Alice:* Didn't you find it exciting when he like jumped off the bridge?
> *Rex:* No, it wasn't exciting.
> *Alice:* To save the girl.
> *Rex:* No. I probably would have—
> *Alice:* Rex, wouldn't you have jumped off the bridge to save a girl?
> *Tess:* You ought to ride out of here on a rail.
> *Rex:* I wouldn't have rode after the girl after she rode up on that bridge like that. He was kind of dumb. He was acting childish when he did that. Gotta try to catch her.
> *Tess:* True.
> *Rex:* She was scared of him. She was pedaling away.
> *Tess:* Well why didn't you like the story, Jasper?

The discussion continued along these lines, with students using their affective response to the story as a means of identifying problematic parts to analyze. Ultimately their personal evaluations of the story led them back to the questions on their story heuristic:

Jasper: So what'd you think about the bike.

Tess: I thought it was cool.

Rex: I thought it was weird.

Alice: It was too small for him.

Rex: Yeah, if I was seventeen, I wouldn't be riding this.

Tess: I would be in the car.

Rex: This is too personal.

Jasper: She was scared too. I'd have been scared too.

Tess: Well wait, what'd she think he was going to do?

Rex: Let's not get into that. You never know. There's crazy people in Russia [the setting of the story] too.

Alice: Well what else does he do that's immature?

Jasper: He chases her.

Rex: We said that.

Alice: What else though?

Tess: Well, he gets this big head when she starts talking about Siberia.

Alice: Well that's his self-confidence coming back.

Rex: That's his self-confidence coming back. You only want to talk about—you and self-confidence.

Alice: Because if he was immature about that he would have bragged about it.

Rex: Yeah, and he didn't brag. He didn't do anything else immature except for hide outside of his house, ride that bike that was a juvenile size for him, quote and chasing after the girl on the bicycle. That's all I know.

Ms. Sanders employed small groups rarely in her classes, and therefore the students had had little experience in working on their own. The prevailing patterns of discourse of the class are suggested by her teacher-led discussion, in which students relied heavily on her for direction and interpretive assistance. It is not surprising, then, that in their rare opportunities for self-directed discussion they struggled. Their most elaborated portion of the transcript came when they engaged in the type of questioning with which Ms. Sanders had initiated their teacher-led discussion; that is, when they responded affectively as a means of identifying problematic parts of the story. What the students seem to have adopted is the use of affective response as a way to identify unresolved portions of the text. Only when they engaged in this type of response did they discuss the issues with involvement and go beyond the most minimal acceptable answers. Their liveliest and most provocative discussion in the small group occurred once they were freed from the analytical task posed by the discussion heuristic. Their small-group discussion raises some interesting questions: How would Ms. Sanders's whole-class discussion have gone had she allowed students to explore their affective responses to the story as the very basis of discussion? Would the discussion have been impassioned and spirited, with wide engagement? Would the students have used their affective response as a way to return to an analysis, as they did in the small group? And if the heuristic had asked for a different form of response, such as to discuss points of the story that had prompted a strong emotional reaction, how would the small-group discussion have gone? The discussions of Ms. Sanders and her students illustrate the importance of attending to the congruence between a teacher's approach and agenda and the tasks demanded of students in subsequent activities and assessments.

MR. AZAROV

Teacher-Led Discussion

Mr. Azarov taught the honors section in the study; his students were therefore more likely to have possessed the characteristics of successful students than were the students of the other teachers. They could be expected to adopt more readily the interpretive processes of their teacher. They might also have had more experience with the sort of formal analysis and argumentation required by the heuristic and therefore might have been well acclimated to the demands of the small-group task.

Mr. Azarov, like Mr. Stone, seemed comfortable with the orientation of the sophomore curriculum. His discussions focused on changes in the characters during the story, and revealed two primary traits: (1) he prompted his students to elaborate on their contributions to the discussion, and (2) he based his discussion questions on student remarks, thus getting into the flow of the discussion and helping students extend their contributions. The sections that follow illustrate each of these traits with excerpts from the transcripts.

Prompting Students to Elaborate on Their Contributions

Mr. Azarov would request student elaborations (coded with "Respond-Request Elaboration" in the data analysis) by repeating their responses back to them in the form of a question, often followed by a specific request for further explication:

> *Mr. Azarov:* What are the key characteristics of this seventeen- or eighteen- or nineteen-year-old boy Costia at the beginning of the story? What is he like?
> *Male student:* He is depressed.

Mr. Azarov: He is depressed? Why is he depressed? Jane.

Jane: I meant depressed more in the sense that he is almost clinically depressed. There is no interest in anything in his life. Pretty much, he just has to be alone. If you looked at it that way, you would say that he almost had a schizoid personality, always wanted to be alone, never find interest in anything family or social. But—

Mr. Azarov: [asks students to speak clearly and minimize noise for tape recorders] You said something interesting about the clinically depressed schizophrenic.

Jane: Yeah. If you looked at him that way, I would say that he did have kind of a schizoid personality.

Mr. Azarov: A schizoid personality?

Jane: A schizoid personality is someone who is so cold and aloof, they can't even bring themselves out of the shell.

Mr Azarov: Okay, so if he can't relate to people, he is in a shell.

Male student: [inaudible]

Jane: Yeah. But still, it seems like she is just this mother figure. He is kind of scared of her.

Mr. Azarov: He is kind of scared of his grandmother?

Jane: Yeah. Like she is kind of turning against him.

Mr. Azarov: She is turning against him? Leslie.

Leslie: It said in the story that his grandmother was the only person that he probably was close to.

Mr. Azarov's method of repeating student remarks as interrogatives appears to have served as a cue for them to elaborate on their replies. The frequency with which Mr. Azarov prompted his students to elaborate their responses is presented in Table 15. He did so far more frequently than any other teacher in the study both in terms of the frequency and the percentage of his total contributions. His *method* of prompting elaboration was quite different from that of Mr. Stone, yet both approaches appeared effective in getting students to extend their thoughts.

Basing Questions on Student Contributions

Mr. Azarov's questioning techniques were different from those of Mr. Harris and Ms. Sanders, who posed questions that pointed to particular areas of the text to discuss and formulated the nature of the inquiry. Mr. Azarov based his questions on the substance of student remarks, illustrating the process of "uptake," which involves "following up on students' answers by incorporating these answers into subsequent questions" (Nystrand & Gamoran, 1991a, p. 264). Rather than using questions to structure the discussion to lead down an interpretive path, he was more spontaneous and reactive in his use of questions, using them to help students elaborate on their contributions and connect one idea to another. The following excerpt illustrates how Mr. Azarov used questions in the flow of discussion:

> *Tanya:* It seems to me like a seventeen-year-old should be a little more like emotionally stable. He was like [inaudible].
>
> *Mr. Azarov:* You think when you get to be seventeen you will be more emotionally stable?
>
> *Tanya:* I'm not going to hide. I don't see, like, seventeen-year-olds hiding in the bushes. They are lonely or something. I don't know.
>
> *Mr. Azarov:* So you would say one aspect of maturity would be emotional stability. Mark, is that right? And he doesn't seem to be there very far, at least when he's at the beginning. Larry.
>
> *Larry:* I don't think it has anything to do with any degree of maturity.
>
> *Mr. Azarov:* Why not?
>
> *Larry:* I mean, also in the household where it is all women—
>
> *Mr. Azarov:* That could drive anybody crazy.
>
> *Larry:* It is different when you are at that age. All you have, is you don't have a male figure if you are a man, and you don't have a reference because you see things a little differently, because men and women have different—
>
> *Mr. Azarov:* Yeah. He has just got a grandmother and an aunt in the house, and he has just lost his mother. It doesn't seem like he ever had a father around. So are you saying you wouldn't call it immaturity? You would call it—
>
> *Male student:* Innocence.
>
> *Larry:* No. I think it is more what is going on in the house.
>
> *Mr. Azarov:* Just a reflection of the life, the way he has been growing up? Esther.
>
> *Esther:* I don't think there is anything really wrong with him like hiding in the bushes, because when what they talk about this, this aunt had like four kids and stuff, and maybe he didn't have his own room to go to or something, and he would like to be by himself. And just like [another student] said, no one knows that he's there till he's picked or his grandma makes a comment or something and she doesn't know he is there. But he can still feel like everything is that's going on so he doesn't miss something.
>
> *Mr. Azarov:* Okay, you are saying he sort of adapted to a strange environment.
>
> *Esther:* We don't know that he is there like all the time.
>
> *Mr. Azarov:* Yeah. It is not like we don't know how come [inaudible].
>
> *Male student:* Do the four kids live in the house?
>
> *Mr. Azarov:* Do those four kids live in the house? She had four kids.
>
> *Chorus:* Yeah.
>
> *Mr. Azarov:* Yeah. I think we assume they must because she is supporting them, right?
>
> *Chorus:* Yeah.

Rather than posing a predetermined set of questions leading to a predetermined set of answers, Mr. Azarov based his questions on students' contributions. His method incorporated the two basic tenets of a Rogerian counseling approach: *listening* and *extending* (Carkhuff, 1969; Rogers, 1961). In letting the students determine the direction of the discussion, Mr. Azarov was listening to them and letting their responses guide the analysis. In posing questions to get them to elaborate on their remarks, he was helping them extend their reflections and reach for greater insights. This combination appeared to be quite effective in helping the students develop their interpretations and participate actively in the discussion.

Small-Group Discussions

Mr. Azarov's small groups did not adopt his specific technique of restating their remarks as questions to prompt elaboration. They did, however, ask each other to clarify or develop their thoughts through other means. The data suggest, therefore, that his method was effective in getting students to elaborate on their responses, even if they did not adopt his particular method. We must keep in mind, too, that as honors students in a competitive high school these students might already have possessed certain academic habits that would make them receptive to their teacher's modeling of interpretive processes. We might consider this factor as part of their enculturation to schooling and as a contributing factor in their ability to internalize strategies and dispositions, particularly in response to analytic questions. The following excerpt illustrates typical student interaction in their small-group discussions:

> *Jarvis:* How does the protagonist change from the beginning of the story to the end?
> *Joan:* This was the what? Oh, the big stuff.
> *Jarvis:* I did not get past the part where he sees the Chalmers.
> *Tammy:* That was weird, I know.
> *Joan:* What's weird?
> *Jarvis:* See, that should change him. That should make him feel that he's not as great because he didn't help her.
> *Tammy:* Yeah, but I don't think he—
> *Joan:* I think he was like—
> *Tammy:* But did that really happen? I mean was he like dreaming?
> *Joan:* I thought it was a dream.
> *Sam:* So did I. I don't understand that.
> *Tammy:* Because we read this last year and we talked about it and I think it was a dream or something.
> *Jarvis:* It was probably a dream.
> *Joan:* Yeah, because the next day they're like oh, you know.

Jarvis: Calm, no show.

Sam: And he just says good night and slams the door in their face. That's not something you usually do, like watch in—

Joan: I know and then he like walks back in, you know, eats a few things, burns his grape stumps. I mean—

Sam: No. He does that first.

Joan: Don't you think he would like call the police or something? Well, whatever. I mean he just walks in, turns the TV off. You know he's totally like nonchalant about this whole thing. I would be like freaking because you know—

Sam: That's you. That's not everybody.

Joan: Yeah, I know but still, what would your reaction be, you know, if like you see this guy with a gun?

Tammy: How does the protagonist change from the beginning?

Jarvis: He changes because he realizes he wasn't as great as he was because I mean he didn't even take the situation. I mean he didn't even do anything with the situation. All he did was say hello, goodbye.

Joan: Hello, goodbye.

Sam: No. We know in the real world, he's not as tough as he thinks he is.

Joan: Yeah.

Sam: He knows now like in reality, he's not as much of a superhero.

Jarvis: He's not as real as he thought?

Tammy: Yeah.

Sam: When faced with a real situation.

Tammy: What?

Jane: He didn't really face a real situation. He faced—

Joan: Well, we don't know that.

Sam: [inaudible]

Joan: He faced a situation where it involved older people that are for him, I mean kids his own age.

Tammy: He could have been heroic. He just wasn't. He was a wimp, kinda.

Sam: When he faced a real heroic—

Tammy: I mean you could have been—

Jarvis: Life and death situation?

Sam: Yeah, he could have—

Tammy: I mean I'm not saying that he should have gone up to the guy and went oh, give me your gun.

Joan: He could have called the cops, you know, or let her in.

Sam: He failed to succeed.

Again, we do not see the specific adoption of Mr. Azarov's technique of requesting elaboration at work, but rather an inclination to prompt one another for clarification and detail. As Table 14 reveals, Mr. Azarov's small groups engaged in relatively detailed discussions of the literature. By prodding students to develop and defend their thoughts through his elaboration prompts and uptake questions, he appears to have fostered in his students an attitude for pursuing their interpretations and challenging their ideas, an attitude likely reinforced by their acclimation to the values and processes of honors-level classrooms.

Discussion

We wish to stress again the exploratory nature of this research, which we feel allows us to generate hypotheses about the relationship between teacher-led and small-group discussions of literature rather than draw conclusions. More conclusive evidence about these relationships can only come from continued investigation into the problems examined in this research, perhaps with larger samples, more long-term analyses of the discussion patterns of particular classes, more diverse teachers and students, and different (perhaps open-ended) types of tasks.

The classes we have analyzed nonetheless suggest some possible ways to account for the processes involved in small-group discussions of literature, particularly the ways in which talk in small groups is related to the discourse that surrounds them. First of all, the discourse of teacher-led discussions seems to influence the thinking and speaking that occur in the small-group discussions that follow them. To accept this relationship, one must infer that the teacher-led discussions examined in this study are typical of the long-term patterns of discourse developed by the participants in the classrooms studied over the first two months of school. Seen in this way, the small-group discussions are derivative not so much of the particular teacher-led discussions under study, but of the greater classroom conversation of which they are a part.

One important facet of that conversation is the frequency of student participation in small-group work. Mr. Stone and Mr. Azarov used small groups at least once each week, thus acclimating their students to the processes and dynamics of the small-group setting. In such classrooms, students have a routine responsibility to apply what they learn from teacher-led discussions in subsequent activities. The students of Mr. Harris, who tended to use small groups for writing rather than literary analysis, might not have been accustomed to the responsibilities of leading their own discussions about literature, which might help account for their abbreviated interaction; and Ms. Sanders's students, who rarely worked in small groups and appeared quite dependent on her for guidance, no doubt were quite unfamiliar with the demands of the small-group format. In discussing the process of small groups, one must take into account the patterns of interaction that take place throughout the course of instruction, rather than simply focus on the small groups themselves outside the overall instructional context.

The research provides additional support for the patterns reported in Chapter 3 concerning the speech genre of literary discussion. The discussion of literature in high school English classes represents what Wertsch (1991) has called an "institutionally situated activity" (p. 47). Wertsch argues that "the forms of speaking encountered in the social institution of formal schooling provide the framework within which concept development occurs" (p. 47) and that experience in certain types of formal instructional settings determines to a large degree the extent to which one will master the thinking and speaking that lead to success in those settings. The discussions of the teachers and students analyzed in Chapter 3 and in this chapter suggest that certain patterns of discourse do tend to structure classroom discussions of literature, with the roles and relationships between students and teachers affecting the ways in which students learn to think about literature.

Our discussion so far suggests that the prevailing speech genre of literary discussions exerts a great power over the ways in which teachers and students talk about literature. Yet the data also show that the patterns of discourse found in the classrooms analyzed in Chapter 3 are not universal. The classes of Mr. Stone and Mr. Azarov departed from those of the other teachers studied in important ways. As noted in the analysis of their classrooms, the discussions of these teachers did not lead students down a particular interpretive path, but rather focused on the process of analysis through explicit attention to analytic procedures, an emphasis on prompting students to elaborate their responses, and the asking of probing questions that moved students to generate additional insights following in their own line of inquiry. With attention centered on moving students to develop their own interpretations and frameworks, these teachers seemed less affected by the tensions that caused a doubleness in purpose among the other teachers analyzed. Additionally, Mr. Azarov did not fit neatly into the dichotomy suggested by the New Criticism versus Rosenblatt contrast introduced in Chapter 1. His discussion was very closely based on the text, yet his teaching did not lead students towards a particular reading of it. His students were engaged in a transaction with the text, yet that transaction involved little explicit connection to personal experiences.

The discussions of Mr. Harris illustrate another variation on the speech genre of literary discussions. Although he maintained the sort of control characteristic of the teachers described in Chapter 3, he illustrates a different sort of response to literature based on extensive reflection on personal experiences. His storytelling approach appeared out of sync with the emphasis of the curriculum and may have helped account for his students' brief responses to the story heuristic.

The classes of Mr. Stone and Mr. Azarov suggest that the greater the degree of involvement in generating the content and process of discussion, the more likely students are to adopt the ways of thinking and concept development provided by their teachers, particularly when subsequent tasks require the same sort of thinking. Students cannot be passive in their learning; along with Wertsch (1991), we question "the assumption that students will automatically come to appropriate instructional questions by being exposed to them in the speech of others (especially teachers)" (p. 142). Rather, students must participate in the generation of concepts in order to adopt the language that explores and conveys them in particular formal settings. Activity, as Vygotsky stressed, is crucial to the process of internalizing both the means of communication and the substance of what is conveyed.

Dewey (1916) argued long ago that teachers and learners should be engaged "in a *joint* activity, as a means of setting up an active connection between the child and the grownup. Similar ideas or meanings spring up because both persons are engaged as partners in an action where what each does depends upon and influences what the other does" (p. 15). He disputed the notion of learning in which "a person learns by merely having the qualities of things impressed upon his mind through the gateway of the senses" (p. 29).

The notion of activity is crucial if the genre of literary discussion is ever to evolve. Berkenkotter and Huckin (1993) describe genres as "sites of contention" that are "inherently dynamic" (p. 481). They argue that, while genre conventions strongly influence the behavior of participants, participants simultaneously constitute the rules of the genre. The relationship is thus reciprocal or, to use the language of Vygotsky, dialectical. Berkenkotter and Huckin focus primarily on mature writers in clearly defined professional discourse communities. Our research suggests that in classrooms this reciprocity takes place only when the students have authority in the discussions. When they simply slot information in the teacher's interpretive text, as reported in Chapter 3, they have little opportunity to constitute the structure of classroom discourse. If they are to adopt the language of discussion and simultaneously contribute to the shape of that discourse, they must be active participants in the process.

We would push the importance of activity one step further. Rather than simply having an experience or participating in a transaction, the students who engaged in extended small-group discussions were involved in difficult *work*. When we speak of work, we think of engagements in which a person meets a challenge with an appropriate degree of skill, as in the state of "flow" which "is able to provide a self-contained little world in which a person can act with total involvement and without self-doubts" (Csikszentmihalyi, 1982, p. 174). The excerpts from the transcripts suggest that, in both the teacher-led and small-group discussions, Mr. Stone and Mr. Azarov continually required their students to develop and sharpen their thoughts. To benefit from the discussions, the students had to make a great effort, pushing at the limits of their capabilities. If students are to be empowered in the classroom, not only must the teacher relinquish authority, but the students must also be prepared to engage in substantive, demanding work. Csikszentmihalyi refers to Warren Ziegler's notion of a "learning stance" and Kenneth Benne's idea of a "methodological character" to characterize those who seek out new learning in their transactions with the world. He sees this trait as offering "the closest approximation of happiness that human existence can provide" (p. 175).

This study suggests that providing a model of response or interpretation without engaging students in the process appears to place too great an emphasis on the role of the teacher in "teaching" and too little emphasis on the students' activity. We recall Dyson's (1990) metaphor of "weaving" rather than "scaffolding," with the emphasis on a transactive relationship. In such a learning environment teachers guide students to the higher levels of their "zone of proximal development," Vygotsky's term for their range of potential in relation to the social context that enables it to develop.

The small groups described in this chapter illustrate the importance of activity on the internalization of new concepts and the adoption of appropriate patterns of thought and speech. The lack of activity of the students in Mr. Harris's teacher-led discussion might have left them only with their conventional role in conventional analytic discussions, which was to slot bits of information into an interpretative text provided by someone else, as did the students described in Chapter 3. When falling back on the prevailing speech genre of literary discussions in their small groups, they took the role of providing brief informational answers to the questions on the story heuristic and then moving along. One possible reason they quickly abandoned their line of inquiry could be their inexperience in the intense joint activity required for effective small-group work, particularly when the teacher's style of response was different from the type of analysis required in the small group.

Our discussion of literary discussion has focused on the use of speech as a means of mediating thought and activity. We wish to stress that we recognize other forms of mediation as well, particularly as described in cultural studies. John (1972), for instance, reveals how Navajo children "learn by looking" and "are visual in their approaches to the world" (p. 333). Philips (1972) has found that for Warm Springs Indians the first step in learning involves silent listening and watching. When we speak of engagement and activity in our studies of classroom discourse, we are describing the specific means of mental involvement that are thought to be appropriate for learning in mainstream

English classes. Studies of other learning situations might more appropriately analyze other means of mediating thought and activity (see Smagorinsky, 1991; Smagorinsky & Coppock, 1994, in press).

In conventional American classroom discussions of literature, talk is the medium for learning a means of response. If the social circumstances surrounding discussions of literature affect the talk that takes place within them, if schools in general and individual teachers in particular encourage specific kinds of talk, and if classrooms are the only place where we assume that discussions of literature take place, then we would be left with the belief that literature is only talked and thought about in limited, and perhaps limiting, ways. Yet the classroom is only one of several types of literary communities. An analysis of other settings for discussing literature might lead to an understanding of other ways to talk and think about literature. In Chapters 5 and 6 we analyze discussions of literature in two such settings.

5 Adult Book-Club Discussions: Toward an Understanding of the Culture of Practice

One of the main reasons we became teachers is that we love to read and talk about literature. But our studies of large-group discussions of literature in literature classes suggest that these discussions seldom feature the kind of talk that drew us to the profession. Although teachers would like their discussions of literature to be free-flowing exchanges of ideas, in reality both students and teachers are constrained in what they say and in how they say it. And our study of small-group discussions of literature suggests that the influence of the patterns of discourse in large-group discussions is so great that it extends to other settings as well. As we have argued in our previous chapters, the patterns of speaking and thinking characteristic of school discussions of literature are not those of discussions we value. It makes sense, therefore, to look outside classrooms for alternative models of how to talk about literature. In the two studies that conclude our book, we do just that, examining in this chapter how adults talked about books in their book-club discussions and then in Chapter 6 how eighth graders talked one-on-one with their student teacher as they read stories together outside class.

Wertsch (1991) explains why such studies might be valuable in his discussion of the tools—what he calls mediational means (see Vygotsky, 1986)—people use to accomplish their goals. He gives the compelling example of the "QWERTY" typewriter keyboard. He explains that the placement of letters originally resulted from the designer's efforts to slow typists' fingers down in order to avoid jams. Despite this history, and despite the fact that other keyboards have proven to be more efficient, the QWERTY keyboard has continued its dominance. Why? Wertsch (1991, p. 37) explains that once a tool has been used for a while, the factors that influenced its design are forgotten and the design becomes accepted as natural or inevitable. We know that we had always assumed that the letters on the keyboard had been arranged to maximize efficiency and had attributed our troubles as typists to unique defects in our abilities. Wertsch argues that what is true for keyboards is true for the tools used in educational settings as well. According to Wertsch, then, educational tools such as grade books, referral forms, anthologies, recitation patterns, and so on are taken for granted as somehow essential to the life of schools. We hope that our final two studies demonstrate that the patterns of discourse in classroom discussions of literature are not inevitable, for as Wertsch notes, "[I]t is often only when confronted with a comparative example that one becomes aware of an imaginable alternative" (p. 126). At such times we often find indeed that the emperor has no clothes.

The growing body of research on situated cognition provides additional support for looking outside the classroom for alternatives. As Brown, Collins, and Duguid (1989) explain:

> School activity too often tends to be hybrid, implicitly framed by one culture, but explicitly attributed to another. Classroom activity very much takes place within the culture of schools, although it is attributed to the culture of readers, writers, mathematicians, historians, economists, geographers, and so forth. Many of the activities students undertake are simply not the activities of practitioners and would not make sense or be endorsed by the cultures to which they are attributed. (p. 34)

According to this argument, then, to understand the culture of readers, one has to look beyond schools. One context that can provide some understanding of the culture of readers and, with that, some sense of direction for teachers of literature is the adult reading club.

The growth in popularity of adult reading groups has been well documented by the popular press. *The Chicago Sun-Times* of March 11, 1990, reports: "These days, it's positively *de rigueur* among baby-boom intelligencia to carve out a few hours once a month to pick apart a piece of literature and a buffet table." And *The New York Times* of March 20, 1989, notes: "Books are drawing members of the 'me generation' out of their urban solitude and into intimate discussion groups. From recent college graduates to people a generation older, these readers are confounding the conventional wisdom that video has replaced vellum." In so doing, they are also confounding the conventional wisdom that studying the culture of readers requires studying the activity of literary critics, conventional wisdom promulgated in large measure by literary critics themselves. In fact, as de Beaugrande (1985) notes: "We must bear in mind that the activity of academic criticism is a very specialized and elaborated domain of discourse" (p. 2), a domain that few of our students will enter.

The Study

A Description of the Clubs

We studied two adult reading groups, a group of six men from the Chicago area who had been meeting for seven years at the time of the study and a group of twelve women from the Iowa City area who had been meeting for three years. To minimize the chance that the groups would change their behaviors because they were being studied, we decided to study groups with whom we had some sort of relationship. Michael Smith had been a member of the men's club for five years, having left it two years before the study when he took a job in another state, and Jim Marshall's wife was a member of the women's group.

The men's club met ten to twelve times a year. Four of the club's six members worked in government agencies, one was a junior high school English teacher, and one worked in health care. All of the club's members had completed college and four had advanced degrees. Only the English teacher had taken literature as a primary area of study. The club had a strong sense of organization and history. Each meeting proceeded in a similar fashion. The host, who had chosen the book under discussion, began by making a brief statement explaining the reasons for his choice. He then posed the initial question. The host had the responsibility of preparing enough questions to keep the discussion moving throughout the evening. On rare occasions the host also brought in information from outside sources.

After sixty to ninety minutes of discussion, the group broke for a late dinner. These breaks ordinarily lasted about thirty minutes. During this time the next host announced his choice for the next text to be discussed. After the break, the discussion would continue for another sixty minutes or so. Throughout the discussion the club members would drink beer and soft drinks (mostly beer) and eat snacks. The host could choose any book, within certain broad restrictions: the book must have fewer than four hundred pages and must be available in paperback. The host could not choose a book he had already read unless it was a book that other members had also likely read, for example, Salinger's *The Catcher in the Rye*. The club had read a wide variety of texts: classics such as Conrad's *Heart of Darkness*, historical works such as McNeill's *Plagues and Peoples*, philosophical works such as Kierkegaard's *Fear and Trembling*, contemporary fiction such as García Márquez's *Love in the Time of Cholera*, and contemporary social commentary, political science, or intellectual history such as Shipler's *Russia*. All of the members were extremely committed to the club. It was highly unusual for any member to miss a meeting, and members always read the text under consideration before the meeting.

The women's club met each month. Of the club's twelve members, eight attended virtually every meeting and four were less regular attenders. All of the members worked in education-related fields or in social services and all had advanced degrees. Only one had concentrated on English as a primary area of study. The club chose its books on the basis of the suggestions of a member who had recently read the book. As Molly, one of the regular attenders, noted, at least one person "should be in love with the book." Meetings usually started with twenty to thirty minutes of social talk, after which the group would begin to discuss the book. The person who made the recommendation was responsible for bringing in information, usually biographical information or book reviews, and began the discussion by presenting that information. This person also could choose to ask questions to frame the discussion. The discussions generally lasted forty-five minutes to an hour, at which point the group shared a meal, discussed the next book choice, and socialized. The group read a wide variety of texts, generally drawn from areas of common interest, most often women's issues, writers of the Midwest, education, and cultural diversity. The group had read a number of classics such as Austen's *Pride and Prejudice,* sociological texts such as *Habits of the Heart* by Bellah and colleagues, education-related texts such as Hirsch's *Cultural Literacy,* contemporary fiction such as Morrison's *Beloved,* and short story collections such as Jhabvala's *Out of India.*

Data Collection and Analysis

We collected two types of data: audiotapes of two discussions of each club and interviews with group members. We recorded the men's group discussing J. D. Salinger's *The Catcher in the Rye* and Saul Bellow's *A Theft.* We recorded the women's group discussing Ruth Jhabvala's *Out of India* and William Maxwell's *So Long, See You Tomorrow.* As in our other studies, the transcripts were divided into two levels of organization: turn and communication unit. We analyzed the communication units by using the same coding scheme we describe in Chapter 2 with only one slight modification. Because the adults occasionally announced that they disagreed with a statement without commenting on the quality of that statement, we added "Disagree" as a category of response. A primary coder rated all transcripts, and a second rater coded a randomly selected 20 percent of each transcript. The raters agreed on 93.6 percent of their coding of the basic purpose of the communication unit, and on 80.2 percent of the subcategories.

All of the members of the men's group were interviewed. Circumstances permitted only three of the women's group to be interviewed, the group's founder and two of its most active and committed members. The interviews were structured around three general questions: how the members felt about being in the groups, how the discussions in the groups compared with other discussions about literature the members have had, and how membership in the groups affected the way members read.

Results and Discussion

The Discussions

Because the purpose of this study was to consider whether these discussions could provide an alternative model for classroom discussions of literature, in our analysis we compare the adult book-club discussions to the large-group discussions of literature we reported in Chapter 3. We do not attempt to characterize the discourse of all book clubs, nor do we speculate on the causes of the differences between the two clubs we studied, although studying a men's club and a women's club may set up an expectation for a discussion of gender and language. We believe with Torres (1992) that such research has become increasingly complex "as researchers have realized that the question of sex or gender differences in language is intimately related to other issues such as race, social class, and social roles" and that "it is now clear that one cannot speak of universal sex difference in language" (p. 281).

The transcripts reveal that the adult book-club discussions feature both striking similarities to classroom discussions of literature and important differences. Perhaps most significantly, the group members share the teachers' goals we reported in Chapter 3: fostering a free exchange of ideas and staying sufficiently on track so that the discussions go somewhere of value. Allen, one of the charter members of the men's group, noted that he values the group both because it allows him to have "open" exchanges with friends and because "the formality keeps [the discussion] to the issue at hand." In addition, the members bring the sort of commitment to the groups that would please any teacher. Indeed, the women's group was founded for just that purpose. As Ellen, the group's founder, explained: "I've belonged to lots of groups and you go in and there are twenty people in the group and five of the people read the book and discuss it and the other fifteen sit and listen to it. . . . It was very frustrating, so . . . we decided to start a group of women who would make a commitment to read the book and come and discuss it." Further, many of the texts that the groups choose to discuss are of the sort that could appear on school reading lists. A closer look at the patterns of discourse reveals additional similarities as well as significant differences. But it is important to remember that the goals of the discussions and the texts, two crucial factors in shaping discussions, are quite similar to those of the teacher-led discussions we reported in Chapter 3. These resemblances suggest that, although classrooms and book clubs are different, the adult reading groups are an appropriate source of implication for teachers to consider.

Table 17

Mean Length of Turns in Communication Units

	Mean (*SD*)
Men's discussions	
Catcher	1.7
A Theft	1.6
Women's discussions	
Out of India	1.6
So Long	1.6
Mean	1.63

Length of Turn

As Table 17 reveals, the average length of turns for each of the discussions (1.63 units) was approximately the same as the average length of student turns we reported in our studies of large-group discussions of literature (1.8 units). That seems a surprising result, for even a glance at the transcripts reveals that group members regularly took turns substantially longer than virtually all of the turns of the students in the studies of both large- and small-group discussions. However, further analysis suggests an explanation for this initially surprising result. In the classroom discussions the turn-taking rules were very clear. The teacher would ask a question, a student would answer, and then the teacher would respond in some fashion or ask another question. In all of the adult discussions, however, the turn-taking was much more fluid. In fact, the discussions were marked by kinds of turns that rarely occurred in the classroom discussion of literature: parallel turns and cooperative turns.

In parallel turns speakers punctuate the turns of others without fully gaining the floor. Sometimes parallel turns featured two speakers alternating, as this example from the discussion of *The Catcher in the Rye* illustrates:

> *Joe:* Doesn't it seem that this young fellow was looking—to uh, to retain the—like the honesty of, a, of childhood and youth, the uh—you know—the spontaneity that, that goes along with childhood, youth and—
>
> *Sam:* I think he was—yeah, I think he was bright and—
>
> *Joe:* And you see, he was right on the cusp. Where he had to, to go in, go over, whether he thought he saw—
>
> *Sam:* You know. He was—he was frightened to, to move on. I mean I agree, with Wallace—
>
> *Joe:* Yeah, frightened to move on, that's right.
>
> *Sam:* I agree with Wallace to an extent. I don't think he's responsible—

totally responsible for his fucked-up behavior. I think he's, a depressed
kid, who is, you know, is having major problems adapting to life. You
know, I don't think it's just a, a function of him being an, an asshole. His
behavior is clearly horrible, you know. But, I don't agree, that he makes
. . . any, that he actually makes a journey. I think he's running in place.
He doesn't seem to go anywhere to me. He's still asking the same
questions, at the end when he's sitting out in California . . . it's like, I was
thinking, this book doesn't really start anywhere, and it doesn't really go
anywhere. I just see him sitting—I see him treading water.

Because the speakers paused to let each other continue, the excerpt was coded
as each speaker's taking three separate turns. However, because neither
speaker really gave up the floor or interacted with the other, the excerpt could
be seen as a single turn by each of the two speakers. More commonly,
however, parallel turns were characterized by short turns from a variety of
speakers interrupting an extended turn by a single speaker, as in this excerpt
from *A Theft:*

> *Allen:* Gina has more wisdom than a sixteen-year-old could possibly ever
> have, number 1. Number 2, I think that Gina—
> *Wallace:* Oh come on.
> *Henry:* Well Gina's twenty-two. Gina is twenty-two.
> *Allen:* Sucks the life out of Clara. You know, on the way going there, she
> is talking about how old she's feeling. You may recall. To this meeting.
> She's talking about her knees, she's talking about the aches, she's talking
> about getting that [since] she'd met Gina. Gina then sucks sucks the life
> out of her in this passage that Henry read on 107. Removes it, but Gina
> as she takes this out of Clara, and passes her into middle age. Then goes
> on, to, to, to give her her child. Telling her the story about her daughter
> giving her this stuff, and then Gina concludes at the end, that now it has
> passed, I've given my, my, wayward youthful, uh, type, of a, uh, image
> and, life to Gina—
> *Wallace:* Yeah, so—
> *Allen:* And my daughter is coming up, having done something that's
> unbelievable to me, and she's part of me, she, she is—
> *Wallace:* Yeah. So are you saying that's affirmative or not?
> *Allen:* Yes. It's definitely affirmative at the [end].

In this excerpt Allen takes four turns, three of them one communication unit
long, yet he is developing a single idea. In discussions with more rigid
turn-taking rules, Allen would have developed his idea in a single long turn.

Cooperative turns are turns in which several speakers are working together
to make a single point, as in this excerpt from the discussion of *The Catcher
in the Rye:*

> *Sam:* It says he hates life, because there's some, there are a couple aspects
> that that, he can't tolerate; it's not saying he has to buy into it, that he has

to *be* phony, but he just won't even participate because there're phony people out there.

Adam: He calls everybody phony in this book for the most part, which is basically, which is basically his, basically he's a teenage adolescent finding things that he doesn't like, so he uses the word "phony."

Sam: He's a nihilist.

Joe: But he doesn't find everybody phony.

Wallace: No. No.

Joe: He doesn't. He—

Sam: People who are dead, not phony.

Joe: That's it, oh people who—

Sam: Children. The children.

Joe: That are children.

Sam: Yeah.

Joe: Nuns—get to be uh, in the non-phony—

Henry: Yeah, the nuns renounced, renounced the world of—

Wallace: The girlfriend Jane, the one he loved so much.

Joe: And it's just virgins, I guess I should just, is what, his virgins are not phony. You know there, but there are people that aren't phony.

From the time Joe says "But he doesn't find everybody phony" to the end of this excerpt, four different speakers take a total of twelve turns, only the last longer than a single communication unit. Yet the speakers are working together to develop a single idea. Because the speech genre of classroom discussions of literature does not sanction this kind of unmediated collaboration, a student would likely have to develop such an idea individually.

We see a similar kind of cooperation in this excerpt from the discussion of *A Theft:*

Wallace: So I, and she goes on—I mean are we, remember this is a woman who, uh, who is uh, tried to commit suicide twice, then she's had, uh, she got a record of difficulties in dealing—

Henry: Someplace else in the book he says that, that Mrs. Wong, Mrs. Wong has given up, uh, on men. There's another place in the book where she, he said that.

Wallace: Right. [all talking]

Allen: She's been married, she had a break, bad, breakup and—

Henry: But but she didn't, but, but the—

Wallace: And she had run, written them off.

Henry: But didn't that, get written off?

Wallace: Yes she had written 'em off. Good point—

As these examples suggest, the existence of cooperative turns, like the existence of parallel turns, makes length of turn a suspect measure of the elaboration that occurred during the discussions.

Table 18

General Discourse Functions in Percentage of Total Units

	n of Units	Direct	Inform	Question	Respond
Men's discussions					
Catcher	2,104	2.4	67.8	7.0	22.8
A Theft	2,051	4.1	66.3	11.0	18.6
Women's discussions					
Out of India	610	1.3	68.3	11.6	18.7
So Long	1,197	2.3	75.8	7.3	14.6
Average	1,490.5	2.53	69.55	9.23	18.67

General Discourse Function

The proportion of the responses in each of the four general categories is indicated in Table 18. The club members made substantially fewer directive statements (2.53 percent) than did the teachers (4.3 percent), although they did make more directive statements than did the students (0 percent). This is not a surprising result, for, unlike students, all of the members of the groups had the authority to make directive remarks, although they seldom exercised that authority. As in the classroom discussions, informative statements dominated the discussions. Much more interesting than the incidence of the informative statements is the nature of those statements, a topic that will be addressed below.

The club members asked substantially fewer questions (9.23 percent) than did the teachers (21.4 percent) and slightly fewer than did the students (14.35 percent). Again this is not surprising, for although the questions that club members asked were important, the discussions did not depend on questions to advance. Teachers use questions to open up the floor to their students, the presumption being that students should not enter the discussion until they have been invited to do so. In contrast, simply being a member of the club authorized the adults to speak. Consequently, the members most often entered the discussion to build on or to speak against the statements by previous speakers.

The issue of authority again appears in the substantial difference in the proportion of responses offered by the adults (18.67 percent) as compared with the students (3.3 percent). Clearly, only the teacher (13.1 percent) was authorized to respond to the statements that students made. As we noted earlier, after virtually every statement by a student, the floor returned to the teacher (see Nystrand & Gamoran, 1991b). In contrast, all of the members of the book clubs had the authority to respond, and indeed they regularly exer-

Table 19

Nature of Informative Statements by Percentage

	n of Units	Logistics	Read	Instructional Focus
Men's discussions				
Catcher	1,434	1.5	2.3	96.2
A Theft	1,360	1.0	2.1	96.8
Women's discussions				
Out of India	417	0.5	0	99.5
So Long	907	1.5	16.4	82.0
Average	1,029.5	1.13	5.2	93.63

cised this authority. The club members spoke directly to each other rather than speaking through another.

The Informative Statements

The general focus of the informative statements is shown in Table 19. For the most part, the informative statements of the adults were similar to those of the students. The vast majority of both the adults' (93.63 percent) and the students' (90.1 percent) informative statements were instructional. In contrast, the teachers made informative statements which had an instructional focus just over half of the time (53.6 percent), with the remainder of their informative statements being comments on classroom logistics or reading aloud from the text. The very few statements about logistics in the book-club discussions (1.13 percent) suggest that the discussions were far more free flowing and far less scripted than the classroom discussions. As such, they resemble conversations rather than classroom discourse. As Nystrand and Gamoran (1991b) explain, one characteristic of conversation is that each turn proceeds from the previous turn. In contrast, teachers who feel a strong responsibility to lead discussions that get somewhere will have to make many more logistical statements to keep students on track and to get them back on track when they stray. Another difference appears in the women's discussion of *So Long, See You Tomorrow*, which included a very high proportion of "read" statements. In this discussion the group began with an unusually extended episode in which they read and discussed reviews of the book. Although the adults generally did not read much (5.2 percent), their reading was often different from the reading that students did in their discussion. Wallace explained this difference as follows: "[R]arely in a class would I get the chance just to read a passage, and laugh about it with my friends, and just agree that this passage is hysterical. Or to take pleasure in various characters and various situations

Table 20

Knowledge Sources for Informative Statements by Percentage

	Personal	Text	Context	General	Prior	Other
Men's discussions						
Catcher	19.3	62.2	3.8	7.6	7.1	0
A Theft	16.1	69.9	5.2	6.1	2.6	0.2
Women's discussions						
Out of India	29.4	34.5	16.9	7.2	12.0	0
So Long	45.3	18.1	6.2	2.0	28.4	0
Average	27.53	46.18	8.03	5.73	12.53	0.05

that are just wonderful moments." The adults used reading as a way to share these passages and these moments.

The knowledge sources that speakers used in their informative statements are presented in Table 20. The most striking finding is the tremendous difference in the number of times the adults used their own lives as a source of knowledge in their discussions (27.53 percent) as compared with the number of times teachers (5.6 percent) or students (9.1 percent) appealed to this source of knowledge. Both the men and the women regularly made sense of the text in terms of their own lives. On occasion a group member had shared specialized knowledge immediately relevant to the situation of the text. For example, only one of the men had attended prep school, and so he could make a unique contribution to the discussion of whether Holden is a typical adolescent: "I mean, I know, I knew literally people, you know that I, I went to high school with, went away to prep school with, that got kicked out of school, did exactly the same kind of stuff." Similarly, only one woman had been to India, so she could make a unique contribution to the group discussion of *Out of India:* "I was thinking about that while we were talking and debating because we were on a bus going into the city, into Bombay, and there was a young woman teaching, maybe it was a little ol—little older, I think, teaching, you know, at the same time babies learn to reach out, and was teaching her how to beg, you know, teaching the baby how to reach out and beg."

More often, however, group members shared more intimate connections with the texts, and when they did so, they took some of the longest uninterrupted turns in the entire discussions. For example, in the discussion of *A Theft* one of the men remarked:

> Bellow was saying that—the whole, Clara is—thinks she found her inner self but she's misled. And that's that's that's the deal, is that we all think we find our inner selves at various times but, we, but we usually find out that we haven't really come right on target. And nobody really, I mean I

know that I don't know the little Joe Richards that's deep down inside me because it changes all the time, and I, sometimes I think I'm right on target, and then other times I realize that I really don't know what's going on.

We see a similar kind of sharing by one of the women in the discussion of *So Long, See You Tomorrow:*

One of the things we were just mentioning in our way was if there are times for all of us that when we were younger we said or did something and did or didn't realize the impact that it had on another friend in high school and I was saying that when I went back to my twentieth high school reunion, I was faced with hearing some things from people that I was—didn't expect on either extreme. One woman came up to me and basically said that I had practically saved her from doom because she was not well liked by anybody and she wasn't in the popular crowd and she was always felt out of it, and now twenty years later she's one of the most gorgeous people I've ever seen, and she said that I was with the popular crowd but that I gave her the time of day and made her feel like something. And then another friend who—told me about a little rift we had and I was not so sweet to her, you know, and she said she was probably responsible but I guess I snubbed her in science class pretty badly but it's really funny and interesting and when you think back I think a lot of his book to me had to do with memory and recall—what memory is and how it changes and what's important about it and what you do about it.

Although not all of the personal connections the group members shared were so elaborated, such remarks regularly occurred in the book-club discussions. As our previous studies suggest, they rarely occur in classes, at least not from students. This problem is especially striking because, as Nystrand and Gamoran (1991b) argue, students are genuinely engaged in reading to the extent that the text addresses questions that students deem important and to the extent that teachers help students relate their readings to their own experiences.

The women's group used their lives as a source of knowledge substantially more than the men did not because they talked about the text differently, but because the women also discussed their experience of reading and their habits of reading, topics that the men seldom addressed. These discussions also account for the difference in the importance of prior instruction in the women's discussions. (The raters coded all discussions of previous reading as prior instruction.)

Interestingly, both students (8.2 percent) and teachers (10.3 percent) appealed to general knowledge more often than did the adults (5.73 percent). This may be a result of teachers' attempting to build consensus by references to media or contemporary culture. That is, if a teacher wants students to have similar understandings of a character, that teacher might choose to relate the

Table 21

Kinds of Reasoning for Informative Statements by Percentage

	Summary	Interpretation	Evaluation	General-ization	Other
Men's discussions					
Catcher	25.3	42.9	7.5	24.1	0.2
A Theft	27.5	44.8	7.7	19.4	0.5
Women's discussions					
Out of India	59.8	29.9	5.3	5.1	0
So Long	68.1	22.1	4.2	5.2	0.3
Average	45.18	34.93	6.18	13.45	0.25

character to a television character because students would be apt to have similar views of television characters. On the other hand, the adult clubs were far more interested in exploring difference than they were in reaching consensus. Cindy, a member of the women's club for two years, made this clear: "You know, it was, in fact, very enlightening to see that other people could read something and be very bright, thoughtful people and get something totally different than I got." If teachers do indeed use general knowledge to build consensus, it is not surprising that the adults made far less use of this source of knowledge.

As Table 21 suggests, there are a number of interesting differences between the kinds of reasoning we observed in the reading groups compared with those we observed in classrooms. The men summarized far less often (25.3 and 27.5 percent) than did the teachers (65.9 percent), most likely because the men presumed that group members had an understanding of the literal level of the text and so had to spend less time developing that understanding. When the men used this type of reasoning, they did so to set up or to defend an interpretation or a generalization. The same was true in the women's discussions, although the high percentage of summaries (59.8 and 68.1 percent) does not reflect this fact. The women's sharing of their experience as readers, a characteristic of the discussions explained above, accounts for most of their use of summary. A statement such as "And when I read it again now, I got a little confused at first because I thought I was listening to the voice of another character" is an informative statement that summarizes the speaker's own experience. Interpretation played an important role in both the men's and women's discussions, as it did in classrooms. However, both clubs (13.45 percent), especially the men's (24.1 and 19.4 percent), did much more generalizing than did either the students (3.7 percent) or the teachers (1.0 percent). The men generalized primarily to inform their disputes about the text. For example, this brief exchange is part of a much longer discussion of whether Holden is an admirable character:

> *Wallace:* We make, we make compromises and we're a lot phonier than Holden—
>
> *Adam:* Oh, and you don't think he's going to make compromises? At sixteen, we were all to some extent rebellious—

Unlike the students in classroom discussions, the adults were authorized to use theoretical speculation about what it means to be a human being. Because the women's group featured more sharing and fewer disputes, they made less use of this kind of speculation.

Responses

The nature of the responses that club members made to each other is indicated in Table 22. Perhaps most notably, in the book-club discussions, members were more likely to signal their feelings about what was said and far less likely to respond in ways that maintained a distance between their personal opinions and what was said. The adults were most apt to make positive responses (48.58 percent) or negative responses (11.1 percent) to other club members, both of which make the respondents' feelings clear. On the other hand, the teachers were far more likely to keep themselves apart from the discussion by simply acknowledging (16.2 percent) a statement, by restating it (38.8 percent), or by asking for an explanation (12.8 percent). In fact, disagreements occurred so seldom in classroom discussions that it was not coded as a separate category. Although the adults (14.4 percent) and the teachers (12.5 percent) had similar rates of elaboration, the nature of that elaboration was substantially different. The adults' elaboration often occurred in cooperative turns, in which members worked together to develop an idea. In contrast, when teachers elaborated on students' words, they most often co-opted them, using them to advance their own interpretation, rather than as part of a collaborative effort. As one might expect, teachers orchestrated discussions with their responses. However, they rarely evinced a personal investment in what was being discussed.

Topics of Discourse

Of course, the microanalysis of the discussions cannot tell the whole tale, for while it can indicate how the group members talked, it cannot indicate what they talked about. The adults' discussions had an ethical dimension often lacking in classroom discussions. For example, both of the men's discussions centered on their appraisal of whether the main character was admirable. Although the women's discussions were less clearly focused, they too were

Table 22

Nature of Responses by Percentage

	n of Units	Acknow-ledge	Restate	Positive	Negative	Ask for Expla-nation	Elabo-ration	Disagree
Men's discussions								
Catcher	481	6.7	8.1	40.7	11.4	2.2	17.5	13.3
A Theft	381	4.2	5.2	47.8	14.4	8.4	11.3	8.7
Women's discussions								
Out of India	114	7.0	7.9	59.6	12.3	0.9	10.5	1.8
So Long	175	6.3	11.4	46.2	6.3	10.3	18.3	1.1
Average	287.8	6.05	8.15	48.58	11.1	5.45	14.4	6.23

marked by such considerations. Allen sees this as one of the great strengths of his group. He notes that the discussions give him unique opportunity to learn about the other members, for in the discussions, he says, "I get to hear them expound on, on moral or ethical views that they, they might not have occasion to cover in our general friendship and conversation as well."

In Long's (1987) study of reading groups, she found a similar focus on ethics. She notes that "for members of reading groups, stylistics and structure matter much less than do believable characters that can provide them with meaningful moral or psychological insights" (p. 29), an emphasis that she argues is at odds with the practices of the academy. Although classroom discussions of literature are likely to be grounded in New Critical practices (Applebee, 1993) instead of the theoretical perspectives in vogue in universities, the excerpts we presented in Chapter 3 reveal that many of these discussions, especially those in upper-track classes, are informed by the belief that structure and stylistics are most worthy of study.

The Interviews

Three themes emerged from our analysis of the interviews: the importance of the social aspect of the clubs, the importance of the equality among members, and the spirit of cooperation that infuses the clubs.

The club members were outspoken in their belief that the social nature of the clubs is an essential factor in their success. In every interview, club members explained how much they enjoyed getting together with friends to discuss books. But the clubs provide much more than simply a chance to get together. Cindy explained it this way:

> So I don't see it as being like a women's support group necessarily, but there's something about it that there is this real feeling of solidarity in the

group that is really special. It's hard to characterize and I don't know if it's the kind of thing that if one of us developed a terrible illness we would all suddenly rally around and be bringing meals on a regular rotation or that kind of support, but you know when you go there you're going to be affirmed in a really, for lack of a better word, special way, and I think everybody there sort of feels that way, or I hope they do.

Some of the feeling of solidarity no doubt comes because some members had been friends before the formation of the book clubs. But some of that solidarity is undoubtedly the result of friendships that formed *through* the book clubs. And even when members were friends before they joined the clubs, the clubs seem to have added an important dimension to those friendships. As Allen noted,

I'm really interested to know what people I like and with whom I socialize feel about a particular book or a particular character within the book. And, and it tells me a lot about my own friends, you know, in the club when they say I admired this character or thought that character was a jerk or, you know, that kind of thing, so, in that regard, that's one of the things that, I get to see, or hear friends of mine, discuss particular characters and why they do or don't like them. . . . Also there's a lot of humor that, that comes out, because people sometimes have perspectives you'd never either think about, or, perspectives that you wouldn't ascribe to them, you know, *a priori,* without having this discussion or this access to the book. . . . I guess if people were to say well what is it about? What do you guys do there? I guess I could say I get to know my friends a lot better through these books and how they relate or react to them. That's primarily, I guess, one of the big enjoyments, and then the, the other one would be again, the, the idea that I get to see their, the perspectives they might take on life's events, within the book, and then relate them to their *own* life's events or experiences.

Because of the nature of the topics of discussion, friendships form quickly, and existing friendships deepen. The club members spoke not only of the enjoyment they took from talking about these kinds of issues, they also spoke of how important it was to talk about them with friends. In fact, all of the members spoke of the importance of the equality of the club members as a crucial feature of the club's success. As Joe said,

It's just, I think it's just from being with people that I've been friends with . . . as opposed to being in a classroom where it's a competitive thing. There's no competition here or anything like that.

The notion of competition presumes the presence of evaluation; a number of the members spoke of the importance of being free from the perceived threat of evaluation. As Henry explained, "I think that when I was a student . . . that if a teacher was running a discussion, that I would probably be looking to try and give the teacher the answer he was looking for." Adam was outspoken in his belief that the presence of a teacher hindered the free exchange of ideas: he noted that the book-club discussions are "better than [college] in that one can speak one's mind freely without having to worry about impressing, or alienating a professor." As a consequence, club members feel free to be exploratory in their statements. As Adam further noted:

> I mean I've always felt, I've always felt I just said, what I thought about a book, or a character. But actually sometimes the positive thing is that I might say something which I think is right. Or correct at the moment I say it. And then people might say something which . . . then I realize that I was wrong. You know if I didn't feel uninhibited, I might not have said the thing out loud, and therefore I may have continued to believe something that was incorrect, that only became apparent to me that it was not correct by saying it.

Sam explained that the freedom group members feel allows them to use the discussion to develop their thoughts, instead of merely stating them:

> I that that's one of the things that I, I really do enjoy about the group, is that people aren't shy; they just jump right in and say what's on their minds. And I think they're not afraid to throw out ideas that maybe aren't fully formed and developed. And that's one of the things I do really like about it; you don't feel you have to have this intricately prepared thesis in order to open your mouth. You can just kind of say what's on your mind, and let it build if there's the opportunity for that, or just let it drop if there's not.

The equality of the group members manifests itself not only in the groups' freedom of expression, but also in the spirit of cooperation that infuses the groups. As Ellen explained:

> Oh, I think that everybody brings in something of interest and you walk away, you know it's one thing to have your own schema or schemata, but to listen to other people's thoughts about it just really I mean, it's like reading a book and you're putting in this part—it's part of the pie and everybody else is putting in the rest of it and then you walk out with a lot. It really enhances what you get out of a book.

Allen echoed this point:

> There are all of these various, you know, four or five opinions that I get, and different perspectives which really enhances what *I* know or see. I get to compare that many more viewpoints.

This cooperation may even extend beyond the club's discussion. Molly explained that she benefits from having her colleagues in her head as she reads:

> Well, I have to back up and say when I read a book for book group, I read it more carefully. I picture all the way through it Cindy will like this—Ellen will like that. . . . All the way through—Jan will really tune in on

this, so that when I leave, I've probably learned some things about the book.

Taken together, the interviews suggest that club members develop a wider variety of knowledge than students typically do in classroom discussions of literature. Probst (1988) identifies five kinds of knowledge that can be gained from literature: knowledge of self, knowledge of others, knowledge of texts, knowledge of contexts, and knowledge of how to read. To be sure, club members gained the kind of textual knowledge traditionally emphasized in classroom discussions of literature. However, they developed the other four kinds of knowledge as well, knowledge that Probst claims is too often ignored in classroom instruction. Because the members felt free to explore their ideas, they learned about themselves. By listening to the explorations of their friends, they learned about others as well, both about their lives and about how they read. And all of the club members spoke about how the context of the club—in contrast to their experiences in the classroom—encouraged this learning.

Discussion

In the conclusion of his article, Probst (1988) wonders whether curricula and instruction could reflect this expanded conception of knowledge. He argues that if they are to do so, teachers must look beyond principles of literary history and the New Criticism in their attempts to devise new curricula and instruction. One place to look is at the differences between the authentic activity of practitioners and what Brown, Collins, and Duguid (1989) call the "ersatz activity" that often characterizes classroom tasks. In fact, the experience of the book club had important effects on the thinking of both of the English teachers in the groups. Ellen, a teacher of English as a second language, explains the effects this way:

> But I've thought about a lot of things that we do in book group . . . and how we do it and I've tried to put that in my classroom. I think in terms of book group and how much more I get out of it when you're interacting with the book and with the group, and that's what I try to do.

Her experience with the book group helped Ellen realize that encouraging interaction is critical if students are to get something out of classroom discussions. This realization is especially striking because of how clearly it contrasts with the practice of the teachers in Chapter 3. Although these teachers also spoke about the importance of both encouraging interaction and getting somewhere, the tension they experienced in trying to achieve both goals suggests that they see these goals as contradictory. In contrast, Ellen's experience in the book club helped her understand that the goals are instead complementary.

The experience of the book group also caused Wallace, a middle school teacher, to reflect on his teaching:

> Well, it's inspired my, it's really expanded my understanding of how I read. And in fact of where I ought to be taking my, my students. Because I understand that even among adults, it's brought back to me more clearly how varied the interpretations can be. And up until my experience, prior to my experience in book club, my experience with other readers was with other English students. Or with other graduate students. And I think they tend to fall into patterns that we all take for granted.
>
> And here I get a chance to see some people who who are adults, and by any standard measure, have to be called literate. They're readers. And yet they can they can walk in, and dismiss a book for some of the most outrageous reasons but you know, it surprises me lots of times. So when I reflect on my students, I'm more forgiving. I have become more tolerant and I've, I've been more interested in getting them to develop their interests, independently. And I'm less interested in, in going after a line. Or a particular interpretation every single time we go out. Than I used to be. I'm less neurotic about it. We still do plenty of rigorous work in class, but I also see the value of establishing—I'd like to establish reading groups. Not, you know, not the traditional reading group, but I've still got to find a way of getting them to work in friendly groups where they would select what they want to read. I think it's a good model. For pleasure reading. And, you know, the leader could rotate. They wouldn't have to, to work the book to death. They could, just come up with some, share some ideas, come up with some interpretations, and move on to another. No, I think it would be a nice catalyst for maintaining interest.

Most importantly, his experience in the book club has convinced Wallace of the importance of ceding some of his authority to his students, something that is essential if the kind of discourse that characterizes the book-club discussions is to occur in the classroom. Students would have to be authorized to talk and respond to each other. They would have to feel comfortable making use of their personal experience, the source of information about which they are most expert. They would have to understand that the classroom is a place in which everyone contributes his or her "piece of the pie," a place in which ideas are developed instead of tested, ideas not only about literature but also about the world. In essence, his experience in the book club motivated Wallace to make his classroom more democratic. Most obviously, this would be true because he sees the need to share authority. But as Dewey points out, creating a democratic classroom requires more than simply sharing authority.

In *Democracy and Education,* Dewey (1916) argued that democratic communities have value for two fundamental reasons: (1) they are characterized by numerous and varied points of interest among members, and (2) they promote interplay with other social groups, in Dewey's view a prerequisite for progress. As the club members revealed when they talked about the social dimension of the clubs, the book clubs developed numerous and varied points of interest among their members, points of interest that primarily stemmed from the group members' using their own lives as an important source of knowledge in their discussion of the texts.

Beyond helping club members develop mutual points of interest, the discussions within the clubs enabled the participants to begin to internalize the voices of the other members of the group. In Bakhtin's (1981) view this internalization is characteristic of what he calls *internally persuasive discourse*. He argues that *authoritative discourse,* the kind of discourse that occurs within schools and other contexts in which power is unequally distributed, "demands that we acknowledge it, that we make it our own" (p. 342). In contrast, "the semantic structure of an internally persuasive discourse is not finite, it is open; in each of the new contexts that dialogize it [that is, open it up to alternative interpretations (see Holquist, 1981, p. 427)], this discourse is able to reveal ever new *ways to mean*" (p. 346).

If our business as teachers is to help our students develop their own ways to make meaning, this distinction between internally persuasive and authoritative discourse is a critical one. As Bakhtin (1981) explains, because authoritative discourse "demands our unconditional allegiance," it permits "no play with its borders, no gradual and flexible transitions, no spontaneously creative stylizing variance on it" (p. 343). Further, it is "indissolubly fused with its authority" (p. 343), in this case the teacher in the school. In short, we cannot expect that students will make the discourse of classroom discussions their own by transporting it beyond the classroom into the other contexts in which they think and talk about literature. On the other hand, internally persuasive discourse is "affirmed through assimilation" (p. 345). As the experience of the book-club members suggests, it "awakens new and independent words. . . . It is not so much interpreted by us as it is further, that is, freely, developed, applied to new material, new conditions" (p. 345).

In a manner of speaking, the clubs also seemed to promote connections between group members and those outside the group, Dewey's second reason behind the value of a democratic community. Because they used their own lives as a source of information, club members began to see the connections between their personal experiences and the lives of the literary characters they discussed, even though the circumstances of these characters often differed markedly from their own. If we regard the literary characters as representing a real community of people—and the book-club members indeed treated them as such—then the book clubs served as the type of democratic community envisioned by Dewey and rarely realized in classrooms.

We are not arguing that teachers should simply make their classes into book clubs. We understand that some of the factors that made the book-club discussions successful are impossible to replicate in large-group discussions in classrooms. The adults all wanted to attend and they brought with them more mature understandings and more varied experiences than our students do. Further, as we noted in Chapter 3, students accustomed to traditional patterns of discourse may resist our efforts to change. And as our study of small-group discussions in Chapter 4 suggests, creating book clubs as one part of an instructional program does not mean that those clubs will be free from the influence of other classroom discussions, discussions that even Wallace admitted are likely to be marked by "going after a line."

However, we *are* arguing that developing democratic classrooms depends in large measure on creating contexts in which students use their life experiences as they join their classmates in constructing meanings. Although this study does not provide a clear answer of how to create these contexts, it does suggest that the effort to create them is worthwhile. This study suggests something else as well: the value of looking beyond our own experiences as readers (see Zancanella, 1991) and the experience of experts in the academy to the experience of adults who love to read and talk about books and to the contexts that support their efforts.

6 Reading and Talking Together: Responses of Adolescents to Two Short Stories

Thus far, all of our studies have focused on describing and considering the educational implications of speech genres. Our studies of a number of whole-class discussions of literature from a variety of contexts suggest that these discussions are indeed a relatively stable form of construction, what Bakhtin (1986) calls a speech genre. Our analysis of small-group discussions of literature suggests that in particular classrooms this relatively stable form becomes even more determined, as teachers' personal styles influence the kind of talk about literature that is seen as valuable. Our study of a different genre, adult book-club discussions, suggests that discussions of literature can profitably proceed in other ways.

Although Bakhtin's theories always stress the importance of the social milieu, he also notes the importance of what he calls "voice," perhaps most easily understood as the speaking personality. In our final study we consider what attending to students' voices can teach us about the ways that people talk about literary texts.

The Study

Students

Sixteen eighth graders participated in the study: four African American boys, four white boys, four African American girls, and four white girls. The students came from four different classes of one teacher. The diversity of the teacher's classes, in terms of race, class, and academic achievement, characterized the entire school.

Each of the teacher's classes was structured as a reading and writing workshop, strongly influenced by Atwell's *In the Middle*. The majority of students' instruction in literature therefore came through their reading of texts they had selected, their writing about these texts in their literature logs, and their discussing the texts with their teacher and student teacher.

Data Collection and Analysis

The study was conducted much the same way as Squire's (1964) classic study of adolescents' responding to short stories. The students were audiotaped as they talked one-on-one with their student teacher while they read two short stories, Morley Callaghan's "All the Years of Her Life" and John Bell Clayton's "The White Circle." Depending on each student's preference, the meetings took place in the library, cafeteria, or schoolyard during class time, study hall, or after school. The student teacher read each story aloud as the students followed along, stopping after each of five segments of the story. At this point, the student teacher asked the students to share whatever feelings, ideas, opinions, or reactions they had to that point. In the conversations that followed, the student teacher encouraged the students to continue speaking through the use of contentless prompts, for example, nods and phrases such as "Anything else?" Before the students read one of the stories, they wrote a journal entry about a relevant personal experience. Although the study was modeled after Squire's, it differs in one important respect: students talked with someone with whom they had a relationship rather than with a researcher they did not know. Because the student teacher would not be assigning grades on this activity or in the course, the perceived threat of evaluation referred to by the adults in Chapter 5 should not have affected the students' responses.

After the audiotapes were transcribed, the students' responses were divided into communication units and coded by the researcher using the same coding scheme described in Chapter 2. A second rater coded a randomly selected transcript from each of the four groups of students participating in the study. The two raters agreed on 100 percent of the general discourse function coding, 80 percent of the source of knowledge coding, and 89 percent of the kind of reasoning coding.

Results and Discussion

Because of the different kind of talk occasioned by this context, our analysis here departs somewhat from the analyses in our previous studies. In the first place, all of the students' communication units were either informative statements or questions, and 746 of the 747 communication units had an instructional focus. (The one communication unit that had a logistical focus was dropped from the analysis.) Second, because we consider the same sources of knowledge and kinds of reasoning for questions and for informative statements and because more than 97 percent of the communication units were informative statements, we grouped informative statements and questions together when we analyzed the sources of information the students employed and the kinds of reasoning they used. Finally, because there were only negligible differences in responses when students wrote before they read, we grouped the writing and nonwriting conditions together as well.

Table 23

Knowledge Source and Kinds of Reasoning
for Students' Informative Statements ($n = 747$)

Knowledge Source	%	Kinds of Reasoning	%
Personal	31.3	Summary	23.3
Text	66.3	Interpretation	62.1
Context	0.5	Evaluation	12.9
General	0.9	Generalization	1.7
Prior	0.9		

Source of Knowledge

As Table 23 indicates, the students based the majority of their responses on the text, as was the case in all of the classroom discussions we analyzed. However, the students in this study made far more use of their personal experiences (31.3 percent) in their responses than did the students in classes (9.1 percent), more even than the average of the four adult discussions (27.53 percent). Interestingly, when the students used their personal experiences, their primary motivation was to help them understand the stories or make moral judgments about the characters, although the format of the conversations would have allowed them to use the stories as springboards to talk about what Squire (1964) calls irrelevant associations (see Smith, 1991a). Lem, for example, used his personal experience to help him understand the ending of "All the Years of Her Life." The story opens with a young man being caught shoplifting by the druggist who employs him. When the druggist calls the young man's mother, the young man worries about the kind of scene she'll cause when she arrives at the store. But he is surprised. His mother demonstrates a "kind of patient dignity," and the druggist fires the boy without calling the police. When they leave the store, the boy attempts to speak to his mother, but she cuts him off saying, "Don't speak to me. You've disgraced me again and again." The story concludes with the young man's realizing the hardships he had caused his mother as he watched her sitting at the kitchen table straining to drink her tea. Lem noted,

> I, I, I like at the ending 'cause it is just like 'cause, um, um, like my mom, she either sits down and watches TV. Like his momma at the end gets something to eat and that's something, that's something to do, right? Like watch TV. That's something to do and fix, um, a cup of tea. That's something to do and, um, like, feel sorry for what I did. And he is kind of like sorry for what he did.

Sometimes the students' use of their life experience caused them to question the actions of the story, as Doug did: "I'm not sure I understand how she can smile and everything at the clerk but when he comes, when they get home, then start getting upset. But still if it was my situation, my mom probably would, like be mad at me and she would probably tell my father too."

Students questioned not only the behavior of the characters, but also the values that gave rise to the characters' behavior, a questioning that was grounded in the values they brought to the story. We see this in Amy's discussion of the mother:

> She is a weak person . . . because she shouldn't, I mean I guess she can worry about her kids and everything, but it seemed like she should have her own life instead of just what her kids are doing. She could, like, she has to learn that her kids' problems shouldn't always be hers. That, if they are going to get into trouble that is going to be their problem and they should have to deal with it themselves. She shouldn't always bail them out and she wouldn't be so unhappy if she wouldn't just involve herself as much in all of it.

Another reason that these students made far more personal responses than the students described in the teacher-led discussions in Chapters 3 and 4 is that they describe their experience of reading, a sort of response that often occurred in the women's book-club discussions but one that rarely occurs in classrooms. Debbie, for example, after reading of how the mother successfully interceded with the employer after he had caught the young man stealing, said, "Well, it kind of shocked me how nice he was being." The students regularly shared their uncertainties, surprise, appreciation, and dismay as they read.

Kinds of Reasoning

The students' interest in understanding the text can perhaps best be seen by the kinds of reasoning they employed in their responses. As Table 23 indicates, 62.1 percent of their communication units were interpretations, nearly 50 percent more than the proportion of interpretations students made in large-group discussions (42.7 percent). Most often the students in this study commented on the characters' actions and the implications of those actions, as students' responses to "The White Circle" make clear. In "The White Circle" Tucker, a boy from a wealthy Virginia family, recalls his conflict with Anvil, the class bully and son of "a dirty, half-crazy, itinerant knickknack peddler." He tells of the time he found Anvil sitting in his apple tree, a tree he had chosen as his twelfth birthday present instead of a colt. In his rage over Anvil's trespassing and his bullying, Tucker lures him into the white circle in the barn with the promise of playing a game. Tucker's father had painted the white circle to indicate the landing area for the hayfork that was suspended from the roof. Tucker tells how he released the hayfork, which narrowly missed Anvil, how Anvil slowly returned the apples he had stolen and walked away, and how he ran after Anvil offering him back the apples. The story closes as Tucker enters the barn and sees "the image of the hayfork shimmering and terrible in the great and growing and accusing silence of the barn."

Many interpretations centered on understanding the characters in general terms, as we see in Debbie's responding after hearing the first segment of the story that Tucker "seems real sensitive." The students also speculated on the characters' motivations, as we see in Jalinda's statements about Tucker: "It's just sort of weird now. Ha, ha. Because like one minute he's nice to him and then the next minute he's all mean and everything. Well, Tucker's like kissing up trying to look like he's going to be nice to him." Some of these speculations demonstrated a real empathy for the characters, as we see in Jerrod's remarks about Anvil early in the story:

> Hm, this Anvil, he, he doesn't want to look like a sissy or anything but he wants, he wants to try to be his friend. You can tell because he says he might play a little bit if it ain't some sissy game. But he said before that I'm too big to play. But I guess he decided that he, if he wanted to maintain the friendship, that he had better go along with him.

Although the students seldom made responses that went beyond the world of the text (only 1.7 percent of their communication units were generalizations), their interpretations occasionally touched on major thematic issues. Jerrod again provides an example in his final remarks on the story:

> And the ending [Tucker] realized that the kid was really in need of a friend and in need of some food, or something. And he just wasn't a big old bully or something. . . . And he's well, felt sorry, he was real wrong to do it. Maybe he thought of all the things he could do if he could go back. He probably could just talk to him. And found out about it instead of trying to do something crazy.

Interestingly, only 23.3 percent of their communication units were summaries, substantially fewer than the average in the classroom discussions of literature (42.7 percent). This difference is even more compelling because 65 percent of the students' summaries in this study were not summaries of the text. Rather, they were summaries of their personal experiences or of their experience reading the stories. In fact, only 8 percent of the total number of students' responses were summaries of the text.

Instead, these students were more apt to evaluate (12.9 percent) the text than were students in our studies of large-group discussions reported in Chapter 3 (2.9 percent). Some of these evaluations were one-sentence endorsements or criticisms of the story. Charles, for example, thought that "All the Years of Her Life" "was really good," while Matthew found it "a pretty weird story." But not all of the evaluations were of this global nature. The students also commented on the structure and the style of the stories. For example, Jill complained about the beginning of "The White Circle": "I mean, you know how a story is supposed to have a lead-in. I don't think this story has a very good lead, since when you read it you think, I don't want to read this." Nate pointed out how he enjoyed "the sentence that takes up most of a paragraph that just keeps putting 'and' in."

Discussion

When the students in this study had the freedom to respond in whatever way they chose, their responses had a personal and moral dimension that is uncharacteristic of students' responses in large-group classroom discussions of literature. The responses of the students in this study suggest that they shared the belief of most teachers that the primary purpose of reading literature is to increase our understandings of both others and ourselves (Purves, 1981). Paradoxically, however, while they seemed to share this belief with teachers, they manifested their belief in language that would not be appropriate to the speech genre of literary discussions.

Their departures may be a result of the fact that the students talked about the stories while they were reading, and consequently they addressed concerns that are seldom considered in classroom discussions of literature. Rabinowitz (1991) argues that, because teachers teach texts that they have read before, usually many times, they quite naturally (and perhaps even unconsciously) emphasize retrospective interpretations, interpretations that seek to identify the patterns that give shape to a text. He calls such readings "readings of coherence." In contrast, when readers are reading a text for the first time, they are much more concerned with what Rabinowitz (1987) calls "readings of configuration," readings that seek to understand what will happen next, readings that Rosenblatt (1978) would call "aesthetic," focusing as they do on what readers are experiencing in the act of reading.

This distinction is important because it offers an explanation for the differences between the patterns of discourse that characterized the conversations that these students had with their student teacher as compared with those that tended to occur in classroom discussions. The classroom discussions centered on readings of coherence. It makes sense, therefore, that teachers emphasized textual details, for readings of coherence are based on these details. It also makes sense that teachers asked students for summaries of the text, for only by eliciting elaborate summaries of literal information can patterns be seen. On the other hand, readings of configuration, the kind of reading most of us are interested in while we are engaged with a text for the first time, make more use of interpretations and life experience. When we predict what a character will do, for example, we base that prediction on our understanding of human nature, on what we have done or would do in similar situations, or on what people we know who remind us of the character have done or would do. By emphasizing coherence over configuration, teachers therefore limit students' opportunity to use their lives as the basis of their readings and as a consequence may reduce the potential for discussions of literature to develop connections among members of the classroom community.

Emphasizing coherence also reduces the potential ethical power of literature. Stories derive their ethical force from the characters' efforts to face moral choices. As Booth (1988) explains, "In tracing those efforts, we readers stretch our own capacities for thinking about how life should be lived" (p. 187). Our living through the choices of the characters is what makes our efforts meaningful. We see this effort in Lem's remarks on "All the Years of Her Life" and in Jerrod's response to "The White Circle." The students in this study seemed to recognize the ethical power of literature. They were actively and emotionally involved in the stories. Unfortunately, this kind of involvement seldom occurs in classroom discussions of literature.

We can only hear students' voices when we allow them to emerge. And if we understand voice as Bakhtin does—as the speaking personality—creating contexts that encourage students' voices presents a special challenge. This study, as well as our study of book clubs in Chapter 5, suggests that, when people talk about literature outside classroom settings, they share themselves in a way they seldom do in classroom discussions of literature. Our challenge as teachers, then, is to foster that kind of sharing in our classrooms as well.

7 Summary and Conclusions

Summary

This book brings together four related studies of literature discussions, tied together by their common focus and by the coding system (developed by Marshall, 1989; see Chapter 2) used in the analyses. The research reported in Chapter 3 analyzed teachers' and students' perceptions of discussions and examined the patterns of discourse in teacher-led discussions of literature in upper-track, middle-track, and lower-track English classes in urban and suburban school districts in order to understand how those patterns contribute to the ways in which students learn to think about literature. The study reported in Chapter 4 analyzed the relationship between teacher-led discussions of literature and the small-group discussions that follow them in an instructional sequence. The research considered the extent to which the patterns of discourse in teacher-led discussions influenced the degree to which students adopted their teachers' ways of speaking and thinking about literature when discussing stories in small groups. The studies in Chapters 5 and 6 each examined a different kind of discussion of literature that takes place outside class: adults discussing books in their book clubs and eighth graders talking one-on-one with their student teacher as they read two stories outside class. These two studies looked at ways of thinking and talking about literature that are not constrained by the conventions that govern classroom discussions.

The research was motivated by three questions: (1) What are the basic patterns of talk about literature in these contexts? (2) What assumptions about teaching, learning, language, and literature inform that talk? (3) What are the important similarities and differences in the patterns of talk and in the purposes for talk in these contexts?

A summary of our key findings follows.

Teacher-Led Discussions

1. In all three ability groupings, interviews with teachers revealed tensions in their ideas about discussions of literature. Teachers in upper-track classrooms explained that they wanted classroom discussions both to resem-

ble a "jam session" and to "get somewhere," especially to a shared and conventional interpretation. Middle-track teachers' responses also revealed tension, but the tension existed because their vision of literature as a unique vehicle for personal growth was at odds with that of their students, only some of whom were substantively engaged with literature. Teachers of lower-track students felt a similar tension even more acutely. Their goal of engaging students with literature on a personal level was often thwarted, both by their students' lack of preparation and by their unwillingness to engage with any material delivered through the school curriculum. For the most part, students' perspectives on classroom discussions of literature paralleled those of their teachers.

2. As a result of these tensions, the classroom discussions we studied did not resemble the visions articulated by the teachers. Instead of the student-centered discussions that the teachers envisioned, teachers controlled the flow of the discussions. On average, their turns in discussions were two to five times longer than those of the students. The nature of their questions determined the nature of the students' remarks. In addition, the teachers tended to provide the context in which students' remarks became meaningful. Teachers would typically weave the brief informative statements of the students into a coherent discourse. Students' turns were intelligible only because of the context that teachers provided for them.

3. Discussions were largely based on the text. On average, roughly two-thirds of the contributions by both teachers and students drew on the text as the source of information. Most informative statements consisted of summaries of textual information or interpretations of the details of the texts.

Relationship between Teacher-Led and Small-Group Discussions

1. Because small-group sessions are but one episode in a long-term process of interaction, they cannot be studied apart from the greater instructional context in which they take place. The patterns of discourse in small-group discussions are related to the patterns of discourse in the discussions that precede them.

2. The manner in which a teacher supports student learning in large-group discussions appears to affect the ways in which students interact with one another in small groups. However, not all of the patterns of teacher talk prepared students for the kinds of exchanges the small-group task called for. Teachers who engaged students in the process of discussion—particularly those whose orientations were consonant with the focus of the curriculum—exhibited several discussion-leading approaches that appeared to influence the

language of students in small-group discussions. The following approaches seemed to facilitate extensive small-group interactions: (1) prompting the students to generate a contextual framework to guide their interpretation, (2) prompting the students to elaborate their responses, (3) building on student contributions to generate questions, and (4) making the process of analysis explicit.

3. Activity is critical if learners are to internalize concepts and processes. The students in this study adopted their teachers' analytic procedures only when the teachers treated the discussions as a joint activity and encouraged students' participation in the interpretation of literature. Modeling a means of response without engaging the students was not sufficient for enabling them to transfer a means of response to the small-group context.

Discussions of Literature outside Class

1. The ways that adults talked about literature in their book clubs and eighth graders talked with their student teacher as they read stories together outside class differed from classroom discussion of literature. However, there were enough similarities among the kinds of talk that occurred and the purposes shaping that talk to make these contexts reasonable sources of implication for teachers of literature.

2. When the adults talked about why they valued their book-club discussions, they talked most often about the social aspect of the clubs, the equality among club members, and the spirit of cooperation that infused the groups. The patterns of discourse in the book-club discussions reflected these values. The adults shared personal experiences, talked about important ethical issues, and shared their experience as readers, all of which brought them closer together. They felt free to offer tentative ideas and to respond to each other vigorously and personally, things they had not felt free to do when they had discussed literature in formal classroom settings. They worked together in discussions in collaborative turns, and the way they read was affected by the interests and stances exhibited by their friends.

3. When students talked with their student teacher outside class, they appeared to be more substantively engaged than the students in the large-group discussions we studied. They did more interpreting and evaluating and less summarizing than their counterparts in the large-group discussions. Their talk was more personal. It also had a moral dimension often lacking in large-group discussions of literature in that it tended to focus on understanding and evaluating the characters' actions, rather than on developing a coherent statement of the whole.

Conclusions

When we read the preceding summary, we became a bit worried. We offer a critique of standard operating procedure. We offer alternatives. We seem to be saying, "Wake up. Fix things." That's not what we mean to say. All of the teachers we studied are very much awake. All believe at least to some extent in the reader-oriented theories we discussed in Chapter 1. Yet their belief that discussions should emerge from students' interests and flow with the authority of students' voices was rarely embodied in the actual discussions that took place in their classrooms. Even teachers who overtly sought to change the nature of classroom talk felt compelled to talk about literature through the conventional language of analytic discourse.

To understand the tensions that force teachers away from their stated beliefs and towards conventional ways of discussing literature, we need to look to the ways in which the speech genre of classroom discussions of literature is embedded in the institution of schooling. Classroom talk is shaped by traditions that are centuries old and held dear by teachers, administrators, parents, and other members of the community (Cohen, 1988). Bakhtin (1981) might account for this wide and often unquestioned acceptance of the way things are by referring to the "great historical destinies of genres" (p. 259) of discourse that govern language in different settings. It is not surprising, therefore, that teachers who seek change are likely to be thwarted not only by institutional structures (Brown, 1991), but also by their own deeply instilled sense of the "right" way for schooling to proceed.

Our research on small-group discussions and discussions of literature outside classrooms suggests that conventional patterns of discourse in classroom discussions are *not* inevitable; that like the QWERTY keyboard discussed earlier they only *seem* right and proper because of their ubiquity. But the salience of traditional patterns of discussion makes it easy for teachers to fall back into them even when they are working to change. Further, because the speech genre of classroom discussions of literature has conditioned the ways that students think about literature even when teachers invite them to respond in new and different ways, students might refuse or fail to recognize those invitations, as we described in Chapter 3. We have all had the experience of leading what we thought of as a scintillating discussion only to have a student ask a question about our "lecture." And as we have argued in Chapter 4, if students are to learn new ways of talking about literature, they must be actively engaged in doing so. Catch 22.

We don't want to end on a note of despair, however. Although we realize that none of the studies we have presented provides simple or clear implications for practice, we think they do suggest a direction that holds promise. In fact, the studies we report here have helped us more fully understand what might account for the potential of instructional approaches we have advocated elsewhere. The influence of the speech genre of classroom discussions of literature suggests that we are most likely to change the way that people talk about literature in school not simply by changing the instructional moves we make during discussions, but rather by devising activities and situations that demand that teachers and students take on new roles.

These new roles require a very deliberate effort on the part of teachers to vest authority in students' voices. The shift in authority must begin as part of a fundamental rethinking of the roles and relationships of teachers and students (Ackerman, 1993). But as the discussions of the teachers we reported in Chapter 3 suggest, this fundamental rethinking may be overpowered by the force of the speech genre unless it is accompanied by an equally fundamental change in the kinds of activity engaged in by students and teachers.

In our own work, we have described ways to change the roles of students and teachers in order to break away from conventional ways of thinking and talking about literature. Jim Marshall (1987, p. 63), for example, has argued that, if we change the writing students do after they have read, we can change the kind of knowledge they employ while they are reading and talking about literature. In his study, he considers the impact of changing a formal writing assignment to a more personal prompt, as in the following two examples:

> *Formal:* In "Just Before the War with the Eskimos" Ginnie's feelings toward Selena appear to change. In a well-argued essay, use quotations and other evidence from the text to explain why Ginnie has a change of heart toward Selena.

> *Personal:* In "Just Before the War with the Eskimos" Ginnie's feelings toward Selena appear to change. Write an essay in which you explain how your own feelings are affected as you meet some of the people who populate Ginnie's life.

These changes may seem minor, yet our studies have helped Jim understand that responses to the two prompts call on fundamentally different ways of thinking and speaking about literature. The changes imply that the rules of the classroom are not those to which students have become accustomed: textual knowledge is not privileged over personal knowledge; coherence is not privileged over configuration; and students must be active meaning makers. And they enable students to break the rules of discourse that govern academic thinking and writing, providing them with opportunities to respond to literature in ways that are similar to those described by adults and students outside the classroom walls.

Peter Smagorinsky developed a different approach to diminish the likelihood that classroom discourse would be authoritative. For many years in his own high school teaching, he engaged his students in drama, oral interpretation, improvisation, role playing, and other forums for talking about literature that did not involve conventional discussion. His eventual reading of Gardner's theory of multiple intelligences (1983) helped him realize that a powerful psychological framework supported such activities. From his reading of Gardner he developed his own repertoire of classroom practices (Smagorinsky, 1991, 1992) in which students break away from conventional logical and linguistic ways of thinking and speaking in their construction of meaning. Most activities he developed involve collaboration among students, allowing them to use whatever speech conventions best enable them to express understanding and communicate. In addition to linguistic forms of expression, the activities encourage students to express themselves creatively and artistically, using dance, sculpture, music, and other media to represent their understanding of issues. Through conducting his study of small-group process and placing it in the context of Jim Marshall's and Michael Smith's research, he has gained a better understanding of the importance of these activities in helping students to shape the discourse of the classroom. The activities enabled students to choose the vehicle and content of their expression and gave their vernaculars legitimacy in "official" school projects. Once students realized the value of their own language in their own activities, their language began to enter into more "formal" discussions, particularly those in which students controlled the floor. Just as the teacher's discourse from whole-class discussions influenced students' discourse in small-group discussions, student-generated discourse in collaborative activities gained authority in whole-class discussions.

Michael Smith (1991b) has described the benefits of putting interpretive strategies at the center of the literature curriculum. He begins his justification for this approach by studying the strategies that experienced readers employ when they read. Our studies have helped Michael attribute the power of the approach not just to the strategies students learn, but also to the way the instruction challenges the relationship students and teachers tend to have with the literature they discuss in class. Michael argues that the texts teachers use to help students identify the interpretive strategies they need to understand a particular genre—stories with unreliable narrators, for example—should not be canonical literary texts. Rather, they should be texts that students feel more control of, texts like cartoons, songs, and brief monologues. He also notes that putting strategies at the center frees teachers from the responsibility of pursuing a particular interpretation, a responsibility that is at the heart of the tensions felt by the teachers interviewed in Chapter 3. Hillocks (1989) has found, in fact, that a strategy-centered curriculum results in classroom discussions which are less scripted than those we studied in Chapter 3, discussions in which students control the direction and the teacher's primary role is to encourage students to explain how they have gone about their journey, rather than to make certain that everyone has arrived at the same destination.

This list is not exhaustive. It is not meant to be. We do not want to seem to provide a recipe for easy reform; indeed, we know that the effort to reconceptualize teaching and learning is great and often painful. We do want to suggest, however, that a major benefit of the activities we have described is that they do not cue the conventional language of interpretation and response. Instead, they place a much greater emphasis on students' knowledge and experience, on what they live through as they read, and on how they talk about their response after reading. What we are suggesting is not so much that teachers resist the speech genre we have described in our studies, though we applaud such efforts, but rather that they subvert it by creating contexts in which it does not apply.

We recognize in making this suggestion that our perspective on reexamining the model of teaching literature that prevails in schools may be at odds with the rhetoric of school reform. Reform efforts of the last decade have their genesis in worries about America's global competitiveness. Our interest in classroom discussions of literature comes out of our belief in the ethical power of literature, a belief in its capacity to help students understand themselves and enter into harmonious relationships with others, the two fundamental goals of education according to Rosenblatt (1938). But as Brown (1991) argues,

> Our goals in modern schooling are far more modest. Perhaps that is one of our problems. Having a very limited, secular, utilitarian view of literacy—as a means to employment, for instance—we have invented a kind of teaching that cuts literacy off at the roots, diminishing both its appeal and its capacity to empower. By focusing on literacy as a practical, technical matter, we have reduced it. (p. 90)

We began this book by exploring the challenges presented by reader-oriented literary theories and by social theories of learning. We close it with a political challenge. We must work to articulate our goals not just in terms of practical and economic benefits, but also in terms of the importance of developing democratic communities in our classrooms. We must also be advocates for increasing the political power of teachers in their schools. As Brown (1991) points out, schools and districts that are farthest along in developing a literacy of thoughtfulness are also farthest along in creating conditions for sustained inquiry and debate among the adults in the system. We know that it is hard to bring the analytical attention we brought to the studies in this volume to our considerations of our own classrooms. We know that as university professors we are supported in and rewarded for taking a critical look at the language of schooling. And we understand that few teachers have that luxury. Yet despite these difficulties, in fact because of them, we remain convinced that changing the patterns of classroom discussions of literature will be worth the effort. We look forward to the challenge.

Appendix

The following excerpts illustrate the application of the coding system. The transcripts are taken from Chapter 4 (see Smagorinsky & Fly, 1993). Each communication unit is identified by the three levels of coding at the end of the unit.

Transcript #1: Teacher-Led Discussion

Mr. Harris: Roxanne, what happens after he jumps into the water? [Question-Text-Describe]

Roxanne: He saves the girl. [Inform-Text-Describe]

Mr. Harris: Is it an easy saving? [Question-Text-Interpret]

Roxanne: No, because the current pulls them under. [Inform-Text-Interpret]

Mr. Harris: That is described in great detail. [Inform-Text-Describe] Why do you suppose the author describes the saving in such great detail? [Question-Text-Interpret]

Karla: [inaudible]

Mr. Harris: It has to be arduous for anything to be important. [Inform-General-Generalize] It has to be difficult. [Inform-General-Generalize] For example, if it were easy to play the guitar, we would all be Eric Clapton. [Inform-General-Generalize] But all of us probably have sat down with either our guitar or somebody else's guitar. [Inform-General-Describe] The first thing you find out is that it sort of hurts and it is hard to keep the frets down. [Inform-General-Describe] So you get one chord and you struggle for a while, like, row, row your boat. [Inform-General-Describe] You got to change it, and it is difficult. [Inform-General-Describe] Now, if it is a matter of just hopping off a two-foot bridge into three feet of water and saying, don't be silly, you're all right honey, that is not going to be something that changes him very much. [Inform-Text-Interpret]

Transcript #2: Small-Group Discussion

Ellen: [reads from story heuristic] "What characteristics does the protagonist have at the beginning of the story that you would call immature? [Question-Text-Interpret] Give examples and explain why they are immature." [Question-Text-Interpret]

Betty: I don't know. [Other]

Judy: Wait, I forgot the story. [Other] Let me get my book right here. [Other]

Ellen: I think that at the beginning of the story, he thinks that to be mature, he's going to be six feet tall, he's going to have arms of steel and he thinks he's going to be in control. [Inform-Text-Interpret]

Judy: He watches TV too much. [Inform-Text-Interpret]

Ellen: And he thinks he's rebelling by eating grape seeds just because his mother is not there. [Inform-Text-Interpret]

Ginny: Good answer. [Respond-Positive]

Ellen: Somebody else talk. [Inform-Classroom Logistics] Does anyone else have any more reasons why he is immature? [Question-Text-Interpret]

Betty: Nope. [Other]

Transcript #3: Teacher-Led Discussion

Patsy: He thought it was mature to, well, he was eating grapes and staying up late with, he was eating grapes and grape seeds [Inform-Text-Interpret] and staying up late [Inform-Text-Interpret] and watching TV without his mother's approval. [Inform-Text-Interpret]

Mr. Stone: Okay, eating grapes and seeds and a couple of other examples. [Respond-Repeat] He was staying up late. [Respond-Repeat]

Patsy: Yeah. [Respond-Positive]

Mr. Stone: And he was also— [Respond-Request Elaboration]

Patsy: Watching TV. [Inform-Text-Describe]

Mr. Stone: And watching TV when told not to. [Inform-Text-Interpret] And all these fall into the category of what? [Question-Text-Generalize]

Patsy: Huh? [Respond-Request Elaboration]

Mr. Stone: These all have in common something. [Question-Text-Generalize]

Patsy: Well, disobeying. [Inform-Text-Generalize]

Mr. Stone: Okay, he was disobeying his mother. [Inform-Text-Describe] All right. [Respond-Positive] Now what can you do with this? [Question-Procedural-Metastatement] In other words, what are you trying to tell us by bringing up these points? [Question-Procedural-Metastatement]

Patsy: That he thought he was mature by disobeying his mother. [Inform-Text-Interpret] He thought it made him a more mature person and older by doing things he wasn't supposed to do. [Inform-Text-Interpret]

Mr. Stone: Thought he was mature through these acts. [Respond-Repeat] Okay, and what does Patsy think? [Question-Text-Interpret] Do you agree with it? [Question-Text-Interpret]

Patsy: What? [Respond-Request Elaboration] No. [Inform-Text-Interpret]

Mr. Stone: Why not? [Respond-Request Elaboration]

Patsy: He was just showing how immature he is by doing that. [Inform-Text-Interpret]

Mr. Stone: And what criterion of a definition of maturity are you using to make this judgment? [Question-General-Generalize] Why is this, you are saying that this is, in fact, immature even though he thought he was mature? [Question-Text-Interpret] That is what you are saying, right? [Question-Text-Interpret]

Patsy: Yes. [Inform-Text-Interpret]

Mr. Stone: Why? [Respond-Request Elaboration] You are saying he is immature because of something and that because is your definition. [Inform-General-Generalize] And what is it about your definition that allows you to make this judgment? [Question-General-Generalize]

Transcript #4: Small-Group Discussion

Alicia: Is he actually immature for these— [Inform-Text-Interpret] I mean, how can you be immature? [Question-General-Generalize]

Patsy: It's, it's kind of like when you're not really mature until you're— [Inform-General-Generalize]

Alicia: Until you're social? [Question-General-Generalize]

Rose: Well, yes. [Inform-General-Generalize]

Alicia: So, a person's shy so they're—social? [Question-General-Generalize]

Patsy: It takes maturity to be social. [Inform-General-Generalize]

Alicia: No. [Inform-General-Generalize]

Patsy: Yes it does. [Inform-General-Generalize]

Alicia: No. [Inform-General-Generalize]

Patsy: Well, a four-year-old is not mature and does she come, or he or she come out and like say, "Hi, my name is so-and-so. Would you come out and play with me?" [Question-General-Generalize]

Rose: Yeah. [Inform-General-Generalize]

Alicia: Yeah, but I mean, no, I don't think you have to be social to be mature. [Inform-General-Generalize] I think there are lots of people who are. [Inform-General-Generalize] But you're not as successful if you keep to yourself. [Inform-General-Generalize]

Patsy: Yeah, but that— [Other]

Rose: But you are not as successful when you are, when you keep to yourself. [Inform-General-Generalize]

Alicia: So you have to be successful to be mature, too? [Question-General-Generalize]

Rose: Yes. [Inform-General-Generalize]

Alicia: Why? [Respond-Request Elaboration]

Rose: I mean, not really successful, I mean, you have to— [Inform-General-Generalize]

Alicia: In what way successful? [Respond-Request Elaboration]

Rose: I don't mean like aspiring, I mean like you don't have to be rich and a billionaire or anything. [Inform-General-Generalize]

Alicia: Yes. [Inform-General-Generalize]

Rose: You just have to like, you can work in a bookstore and be successful— [Inform-General-Generalize] I mean, it depends on what your standards are. [Inform-General-Generalize]

Alicia: Yeah but if you worked in a bookstore and you were shy and you were antisocial, you're still not mature? [Question-General-Generalize]

Rose: You really wouldn't be. [Inform-General-Generalize]

Alicia: Why? [Respond-Request Elaboration] Yeah, but I don't understand why. [Respond-Request Elaboration]

References

Ackerman, J. (1993). The promise of writing to learn. *Written Communication, 10*(3), 334–370.

Amidon, E., & Flanders, N. (1963). *The role of the teacher in the classroom.* Minneapolis: Paul S. Amidon.

Applebee, A. N. (1989). *The teaching of literature in programs with reputations for excellence in English* (Technical Report No. 1.1). Albany: University at Albany, State University of New York, Center for the Learning and Teaching of Literature.

———. (1993). *Literature in the secondary school: Studies of curriculum and instruction in the United States.* NCTE Research Report No. 25. Urbana, IL: National Council of Teachers of English.

Atwell, N. (1987). *In the middle: Writing, reading, and learning with adolescents.* Portsmouth, NH: Boynton/Cook.

Bakhtin, M. M. (1981). *The dialogic imagination: Four essays by M. M. Bakhtin.* Austin: University of Texas Press.

———. (1984). *Problems of Dostoevsky's poetics.* Minneapolis: University of Minnesota Press.

———. (1986). *Speech genres and other late essays.* Austin: University of Texas Press.

Barnes, D. (1969). Language in the secondary classroom. In D. Barnes, J. Britton, & H. Rosen (Eds.), *Language, the learner, and the school.* New York: Harmondsworth.

Bauman, R., & Sherzer, J. (Eds.). (1974). *Explorations in the ethnography of speaking.* New York: Cambridge University Press.

de Beaugrande, R. (1985). Poetry and the ordinary reader: A study of immediate responses. *Empirical Studies of the Arts, 3,* 1–21.

Bellack, A., Kleibard, H., Hyman, R., & Smith, F. (1966). *The language of the classroom.* New York: Teachers College Press.

Berger, P. L., & Luckmann, T. (1966). *The social construction of reality: A treatise in the sociology of knowledge.* New York: Anchor.

Berkenkotter, C., & Huckin, T. N. (1993). Rethinking genre from a sociocognitive perspective. *Written Communication, 10*(4), 475–509.

Bleich, D. (1975). *Readings and feelings.* Urbana, IL: National Council of Teachers of English.

Bloom, B. (1954). The thought process of students in discussion. In S. J. French (Ed.), *Accent on teaching: Experiments in general education* (pp. 23–46). New York: Harper and Brothers.

Booth, W. (1988). *The company we keep.* Berkeley: University of California Press.

Brooks, C., & Warren, R. P. (1938). *Understanding poetry.* New York: Henry Holt.

Brown, J. S., Collins, J., & Duguid, P. (1989). Situated cognition and the culture of learning. *Educational Researcher, 18,* 32–42.

Brown, R. (1991). *Schools of thought: How the politics of literacy shape thinking in the classroom.* San Francisco: Jossey-Bass.

Bruner, J. (1975). From communication to language: A psychological perspective. *Cognition, 3,* 255–287.

Bruner, J., & Olson, D. R. (1980). Symbols and texts as tools of thought. *Interchange, 8,* 1–15.

Carkhuff, R. R. (1969). *Helping and human relations: A primer for lay and professional helpers. Vol. 1. Selection and training.* New York: Holt, Rinehart & Winston.

Cazden, C. B. (1979). Peekaboo as an instructional model: Discourse development at home and at school. *Papers and Reports on Child Language Development, 17,* 1–19.

————. (1988). *Classroom discourse: The language of teaching and learning.* Portsmouth, NH: Heinemann.

Cohen, D. K. (1988). Plus que ça change . . . In P. Jackson (Ed.), *Contributing to educational change: Perspectives on research and practice.* Berkeley, CA: McCutcheon.

Csikszentmihalyi, M. (1982). Learning, "flow," and happiness. In R. Gross (Ed.), *Invitation to lifelong learning* (pp. 167–187). Chicago: Follett.

Csikszentmihalyi, M., & Larson, R. (1984). *Being adolescent: Conflict and growth in the teenage years.* New York: Basic Books.

Csikszentmihalyi, M., Rathunde, K., & Wahlaen, S. (1993). *Talented teenagers.* New York: Cambridge University Press.

Culler, J. (1980). Prologomena to a theory of reading. In S. R. Suleiman & I. Crosman (Eds.), *The reader in the text* (pp. 46–66). Princeton, NJ: Princeton University Press.

Dewey, J. (1916). *Democracy and education: An introduction to the philosophy of education.* New York: Free Press.

Dillon, J. T., & Searle, D. (1981). The role of language in one first-grade classroom. *Research in the Teaching of English, 15,* 311–328.

DiPardo, A., & Freedman, S. W. (1987). Historical overview: Groups in the writing classroom (Technical Report No. 4). Berkeley, CA: Center for the Study of Writing.

————. (1988). Peer response groups in the writing classroom: Theoretic foundations and new directions. *Review of Educational Research, 58*(2), 119–149.

Dyson, A. H. (1990). Weaving possibilities: Rethinking metaphors for early literacy development. *The Reading Teacher, 44*(3), 202–213.

Eagleton, T. (1983). *Literary theory: An introduction.* Minneapolis: University of Minnesota Press.

Fetterley, J. (1978). *The resisting reader: A feminist approach to American fiction.* Bloomington: Indiana University Press.

Fish, S. (1980). *Is there a text in this class?* Cambridge, MA: Harvard University Press.

Gardner, H. (1983). *Frames of mind.* New York: Basic Books.

Gates, H. L. (1988). *The signifying monkey: A theory of Afro-American literary criticism.* New York: Oxford University Press.

Goodlad, J. I. (1984). *A place called school: Prospects for the future.* New York: McGraw-Hill.

Graff, G. (1990, April). Debate in the canon class. *Harper's Magazine,* 31–35.

Heath, S. B. (1983). *Ways with words: Language, life, and work in communities and classrooms.* Cambridge: Cambridge University Press.

Hillocks, G. (1986). *Research on written composition: New directions in teaching.* Urbana, IL: ERIC and the National Conference on Research in English.

———. (1989). Literary texts in classrooms. In P. W. Jackson & S. Haroutunian-Gordon (Eds.), *From Socrates to software: The teacher as text and the text as teacher. 88th yearbook of the National Society for the Study of Education* (pp. 135–158). Chicago: University of Chicago Press.

Hillocks, G., & Ludlow, L. (1984). A taxonomy of skills in reading and interpreting fiction. *American Journal of Educational Research, 21,* 7–24.

Hoetker, J., & Ahlbrand, W. P. 1969. The persistence of the recitation. *American Educational Research Journal, 6,* 145–167.

Holland, N. (1975). *Five readers reading.* New York: Yale University Press.

Holquist, M. (Ed.). (1981). *The dialogic imagination: Four essays by M. M. Bakhtin.* Austin: University of Texas Press.

John, V. P. (1972). Styles of learning—styles of teaching: Reflections on the education of Navajo children. In C. B. Cazden, V. P. John & D. Hymes (Eds.), *Functions of language in the classroom* (pp. 331–343). New York: Teachers College Press.

Kirkpatrick, C. G. (1972). *The college literature class: Observation and description of class sessions on* The Scarlet Letter. (ERIC Document Reproduction Service No. ED 070 098)

Lee, C. D. (1993). *Signifying as a scaffold for literary interpretation: The pedagogical implications of an African American discourse genre.* NCTE Research Report No. 26. Urbana, IL: National Council of Teachers of English.

Long, E. (1987). Reading groups and the postmodern crisis of cultural authority. *Cultural Studies, 1*(3), 29–50.

Mailloux, S. (1982). *Interpretive conventions.* Ithaca, NY: Cornell University Press.

March, F. A. (1893). Recollections of language teaching. *PMLA 25.*

Marshall, J. D. (1987). The effects of writing on students' understanding of literary texts. *Research in the Teaching of English, 21*(1), 30–63.

———. (1989). Patterns of discourse in classroom discussion of literature. Albany, NY: Center for the Learning and Teaching of Literature.

McMahon, S. (1991, April). *Book club: How written and oral discourse influence the development of ideas as children respond to literature.* Paper presented at the annual meeting of the American Educational Research Association, Chicago.

Mehan, H. (1979). *Learning lessons.* Cambridge, MA: Harvard University Press.

———. (1982). The structure of classroom events and their consequences for student performance. In P. Gilmore & A. A. Glatthorn (Eds.), *Children in and out of school: Ethnography and education* (pp. 59–87). Washington, DC: Center for Applied Linguistics.

Nystrand, M., & Gamoran, A. (1991a). Instructional discourse, student engagement and literature achievement. *Research in the Teaching of English, 25*(3), 261–290.

———. (1991b). Student engagement: When recitation becomes conversation. In H. Waxman & H. Wallberg (Eds.), *Contemporary research on teaching* (pp. 257–276). Berkeley, CA: McCutcheon.

Ohmann, R. M. (1976). *English in America: A radical view of the profession.* New York: Oxford University Press.

Philips, S. U. (1972). Participant structures and communicative competence: Warm Springs children in community and classroom. In C. B. Cazden, V. P. John, & D. Hymes (Eds.), *Functions of language in the classroom.* New York: Teachers College Press.

Probst, R. (1988). Readers and literary texts. In B. Nelms (Ed.), *Literature in the classroom: Readers, texts, and contexts* (pp. 19–29). Urbana, IL: National Council of Teachers of English.

Purves, A. (1981). *Reading and literature: American achievement in international perspective.* Urbana, IL: National Council of Teachers of English.

Rabinowitz, P. (1987). *Before reading.* Ithaca, NY: Cornell University Press.

———. (1991, February). *A thousand times and never like: Re-reading for class.* Paper presented at the midwinter meeting of the National Council of Teachers of English Assembly for Research, Chicago.

Rogers, C. (1961). *On becoming a person.* Boston: Houghton-Mifflin.

Rosenblatt, L. (1938). *Literature as exploration.* New York: Noble & Noble.

———. (1978). *The reader, the text, the poem: The transactional theory of the literary work.* Carbondale: Southern Illinois University Press.

Scholes, R. (1985). *Textual power: Literary theory and the teaching of English.* New Haven, CT: Yale University Press.

Sinclair, J., & Coulthard, R. (1975). *Towards an analysis of discourse: The English used by teachers and pupils.* London: Oxford University Press.

Slavin, R. (1989). Research on cooperative learning: An international perspective. *Scandinavian Journal of Educational Research, 33*(4), 231–243.

Smagorinsky, P. (1991). *Expressions: Multiple intelligences in the English class.* Urbana, IL: National Council of Teachers of English.

———. (1992). Reconfiguring the English classroom for multiple intelligences. In J. L. Collins (Ed.), *Vital signs 3: Restructuring the English classroom* (pp. 35–44). Portsmouth, NH: Heinemann Boynton/Cook.

Smagorinsky, P., & Coppock, J. (1994). Cultural tools and the classroom context: An exploration of an artistic response to literature. *Written Communication, 11*(3), 283–310.

———. (in press). Exploring an evocation of the literary work: Processes and possibilities of an artistic response to literature. In K. Gill (Ed.), *Arts in the language arts.* Urbana, IL: National Council of Teachers of English.

Smagorinsky, P., & Fly, P. K. (1993). The social environment of the classroom: A Vygotskian perspective on small group process. *Communication Education, 42*(2), 159–171.

Smith, M. W. (1991a). Constructing meaning from text: An analysis of ninth-grade reader response. *Journal of Educational Research, 84*, 263–272.

————. (1991b). *Understanding unreliable narrators.* Urbana, IL: National Council of Teachers of English.

Squire, J. (1964). *Responses of adolescents while reading four short stories.* Urbana, IL: National Council of Teachers of English.

Stodolsky, S. (1984). Frameworks for studying instructional processes in peer workgroups. In P. Peterson, L. Wilkinson, & M. Hallinan (Eds.), *The social context of instruction: Group organization and group processes.* New York: Academic Press.

Tompkins, J. (1985). *Sensational designs: The cultural work of American fiction, 1790–1860.* New York: Oxford University Press.

Torres, L. (1992). Women and language: From sex differences to power dynamics. In C. Kramarae & D. Spender (Eds.), *The knowledge explosion: Generations of feminist scholarship.* New York: Teachers College Press.

Vygotsky, L. (1978). *Mind in society: The development of higher psychological processes.* M. Cole, J. Scribner, V. John-Steiner, & E. Souberman (Eds.). Cambridge, MA: Harvard University Press.

————. (1986). *Thought and language.* Cambridge, MA: MIT Press.

Wertsch, J. V. (Ed.). (1985). *Culture, communication, and cognition: Vygotskian perspectives.* New York: Cambridge University Press.

————. (1991). *Voices of the mind: A sociocultural approach to mediated action.* Cambridge, MA: Harvard University Press.

Zancanella, D. (1991). Teachers reading/readers teaching: Five teachers' personal approaches to literature and their teaching of literature. *Research in the Teaching of English, 25,* 5–33.

Index

Authors

James D. Marshall is associate professor of English and English education at the University of Iowa, where he directs the General Education Literature Program. Having taught high school English for six years, he is interested in the relationships between writing and literary understanding among secondary students and in the ways that literature is discussed in classrooms. His publications include research reports in *Research in the Teaching of English; Ways of Knowing: Research and Practice in the Teaching of Writing*, with James Davis; and *Teaching Literature in the Secondary School*, with Richard Beach. He is chair of NCTE's Standing Committee on Research and executive secretary of the High School Task Force for the Standards Project in English Language Arts. He has won the James N. Murray Award for Faculty Excellence and the University of Iowa's Outstanding Teaching Award.

Peter Smagorinsky teaches English education at the University of Oklahoma. While teaching high school English from 1977 to 1990, he developed an interest in how literacy is defined in classrooms. He is now pursuing this area of inquiry in studies of how students construct meaning in English classes and across the curriculum. His recent publications include *Expressions: Multiple Intelligences in the English Class, Speaking about Writing: Reflections on Research Methodology*, and articles in various journals. He is currently a member of the executive board of the Oklahoma Council of Teachers of English and serves on NCTE's Standing Committee on Research.

Michael W. Smith teaches English education in the Literacy Cluster of Rutgers University's Graduate School of Education. His research interests, which he developed while teaching high school English for eleven years, center around the knowledge and attitudes that experienced readers bring to texts and how teachers can use that understanding to help students have more meaningful transactions when they read. His publications include *Reducing Writing Apprehension* and *Understanding Unreliable Narrators: Reading between the Lines in the Literature Classroom,* numerous journal articles, and chapters in edited collections. He is currently co-associate chair of NCTE's Assembly for Research and is on the Standing Committee on Research.

Collaborators

Helen Dale is assistant professor of English at the University of Wisconsin–Eau Claire and director of the West Central Wisconsin Writing Project. She has taught high school English and works with preservice teachers. Her research interest is in collaborative writing, about which she writes and makes presentations.

Richard H. Fehlman is assistant professor of English education at the University of Northern Iowa and was a high school English teacher for more than twenty years. In addition to writing journal articles and book chapters, he chairs NCTE's Assembly on Media Arts and is at present working on a book about movie pedagogy, *Processing Film: Reasoning with Students about Movies.* He makes presentations regularly at NCTE conventions and affiliate conferences and is editor of the *Iowa English Bulletin.*

Pamela K. Fly is an instructor in the College of Education at the University of Oklahoma and works with student teachers and clinical instructors through the Office of Field Experiences. She received her Ph.D. degree in English education from the University of Oklahoma in 1994. Her recent publications include an article, with Peter Smagorinsky, "The Social Environment of the Classroom: A Vygotskian Perspective on Small Group Process" in *Communication Education.* She taught high school English and was a librarian for ten years in Missouri and Arkansas.

Ruth A. Frawley teaches sixth-, seventh-, and eighth-grade English in Madison, Wisconsin. A member of NCTE and the Wisconsin Council of Teachers of English, she is completing her master's degree in curriculum and instruction at the University of Wisconsin–Madison.

Suzanne E. Gitomer teaches eighth-grade English at Round Valley Middle School in Clinton Township, New Jersey. She received her master's degree in English education from Rutgers University in 1993.

Mary Beth Hines is assistant professor at Indiana University, where she teaches courses in English education. She has taught and conducted research in high school and college English classes. She is currently exploring how pedagogical frameworks developed with feminism, Marxism, and reader-response theories might concurrently enrich classroom inquiry as they promote social justice.

David E. Wilson is associate professor of education and English at the University of Nebraska–Lincoln. He has taught English and journalism in public and private high schools in Afghanistan, Missouri, Pennsylvania, and Iowa. In addition to journal articles and book chapters, he has authored *Attempting Change: Teachers Moving from Writing Project to Classroom Practice.* His recent work with Joy Ritchie focuses on the uses of narrative and the development of understandings of English, as well as teaching preservice English teachers.

Titles in the NCTE Research Report Series

NCTE began publishing the Research Report series in 1963 with *The Language of Elementary School Children*. Volumes 4–6, 8–12, 14, 17, 20, and 21 are out of print. The following titles are available through the NCTE *Catalog*.